More advance praise for Embedded in Clay:

"These stories about Clay inhabitants captivate and lure one in. I wanted to see, feel, taste, and touch through these local heroes. The authors imbued the work with dialect, empathy, history, and humor. Not living in Florida, I enjoyed looking up each locale on a map to further dip into the legacy of Clay."

Shonnie Brown, M.A., writer, editor, visual artist, Healdsburg, California

"Ever heard of the 'Water Dogs' of Black Creek? Martha Chalker of Middleburg? Or Augusta Fells Savage of Green Cove Springs? How about Bokar of the Monkey Farm? Or Frank Towers in Camp Blanding? These and other unique characters leap from the pages of *Embedded in Clay* to hint at horizons of history in northeast Florida. Some remained in Clay County their entire lives; some traveled worldwide. All are worthy of our glances into the past. As you read, you see the creek, soak in its darkness, or revel in its neighbors' triumphs. Find a deeper appreciation of this place as you learn more about its individuals. The stories bring delight and joy to readers."

Bobbi McDermott, engineer and former Orange Park High School physics and chemistry teacher

"As a Clay County resident for over three decades, I'd grown immune to its natural beauty, quirky characters, and unique history. *Embedded in Clay* transported me to the dark waters of Black Creek. I marveled at the history of artist Augusta

Savage and the beauty of her works, and I enjoyed the story of the chimpanzees at the Monkey Farm."

Ron Word, retired wire service correspondent

"When brought face to face with [the train], Frank Towers seized the moment in history and became a messenger of providence and sustenance to the desperately sick Jews. Long after the war, he continued to reunite veterans and Holocaust survivors around the world to tell their stories. As American Jews, we felt touched by his compassion and regret we didn't meet him."

Gary and Penina Weltman, Jacksonville, Florida

"These stories taught me a great deal about where I grew up, yet knew little about. Born and raised in Jacksonville, my dad and I went fishing on Black Creek, one of his favorite places. I loved the story and could see that dark water and feel the cool mud on my feet. What strong pictures it paints of life long ago."

Linda M. Ashley, LMSW, Winthrop University,
Social Work Department, retired

"The story about Martha Chalker was lyrical and informative. Paula Hilton's story about Augusta Fells Savage was inspirational! I knew Savage was an artist of the Harlem Renaissance, but had no idea about her rough family life or her interesting academic background. Learning she grew up in Green Cove Springs makes me proud to call Clay County home. Tim Gilmore's article about the monkey farm in Orange Park was so intriguing! I will never pass by The Granary without thinking about the Humanzee."

Beverly Kay Suits, English teacher

"A priceless memoir of a World War II Army officer's experience after rescuing Jews from a Nazi death train. It reshaped his world. Frank Towers trained at Camp Blanding and [later] returned to help found the military museum there. I once visited with other Penney Farms residents and we were fortunate: Captain Frank was our tour guide."

Dee Yurdock, LNCS, USNR

"In the Clay of her birthplace, where many would see only mud, Augusta Fells Savage saw nascent beauty, emotion, power, and potential trapped and was compelled to set it free. We see how she persevered and rose above the obstacles and unfairness to become a successful and recognized sculptor. She did not hoard her talent, but unselfishly and freely (often literally) shared with others through teaching and mentoring. Truly she was a role model for those around her."

Julie Pipho, teacher, proofreader for international courts

"In 'The Bardin Booger Unmasked,' Lena Crain gives us an interesting insight into the back story of Florida's own bigfoot. She shows how even a small town with a little-known myth can make an impact on people's lives. 'Blondie and the Bardin Booger' by Lillian Brown is a wonderful bedtime story to share with siblings or children."

Victoria VanDuzee, student, Clay County

"Thank you for reminding us our little patch of earth here nurtured amazing Floridians, from world-renown sculptor Augusta Fells Savage and WWII Holocaust liberator Frank Towers to the 'everyday' people who lived full, rich lives without ever leaving Florida, 'water dogs,' piney-woods pioneers, men and women we proudly call our ancestors, family, friends, and most aptly—our neighbors—in Clay County."

Janet Withers,
NE Florida native, eco-tourism/history advocate;
program coordinator, Dig Local Network Farmers Markets

"Maude Burroughs Jackson is an oral historian who won't allow her heritage to go by the wayside. Through Jung's pen, Maude reveals the strength and determination of those who endured a period when racial inequality ran rampant in the small towns of Florida. The struggle and hardship were certainly real and deserve to be told."

K.I. Knight, author of the national award-winning
historical series, Fate & Freedom

"Diane Shepard's pieces immediately thrust readers into the shoes of historic Clay residents. Her vivid imagery shows us through their eyes the beautiful and sometimes difficult life along Black Creek and in rural Clay County."

Tonya Hull, 20-year resident on Black Creek,
English/reading teacher

Embedded in Clay

A County in Northeast Florida

Clay County Writers Group

of the Florida Writers Association, Inc.

Orange Park, Florida

Project director and co-editor: Maureen A. Jung, Ph.D.

Editor: Lynn Skapyak Harlin

ISBN: 978-0-9861109-6-2

Library of Congress Control Number: 2018962216

Second Printing

Publisher: Clay County Writers, Orange Park, Florida, a group sponsored by the Florida Writers Association, Inc.

Printed in the United States of America.

Cover design: Kathleen Walls
Interior design: Carrie Richter, The Monkey Factory

For more information:

Visit EmbeddedinClay.com or FloridaWriters.net

Dedication

To the memory of the Shantyboat, blown to bits during Hurricane Irma while docked on the Trout River north of Jacksonville. Home to Lynn Skapyak Harlin's Shantyboat Writing Workshops, the rickety structure weathered the storms of more than 16 years. During that time, over 700 participants found their way to the vessel.

Writers of all kinds traveled to the Shantyboat to improve their skills, as Lynn challenged them do their best work. Though the boat is lost, few who descended its rickety gangway will ever forget the experience. The Shantyboat lives on in the stories, photos, learning, and laughter of all who passed through her doors.

Embedded (adjective)*

1. fixed firmly and deeply in a surrounding solid mass.
2. constituting a permanent and noticeable feature of something.
3. journalism assigned to accompany an active military unit.
4. grammar inserted into a sentence
5. computing (of a piece of software) made an integral part of other software.

* Some emphasis in original.
https://collinsdictionary.com/us/dictionary/english/embedded

Acknowledgments

In gratitude to our community for sharing memories, insights, financial resources, and connections that made this project possible: Brenda Barclay, Kathy Barnett, Alice and Bill Basford, Jack Basford, Jeff Basford, Mike Basford, Black Heritage Museum, Shonnie Brown, Jon Cantrell, City of Jacksonville, *Clay Leader*, *Clay Today*, the CalaVida Arts Festival, Camp Blanding Museum, Chris Coward, Chrissy Jackson, Carol Jones, Clay County Archives, Clay County County Public Libraries, Doug Conkey, Ed and Frances Dickson, Beth Eifert, *The Florida Times-Union*, *The Florida Writer*, Florida Writers Association, Inc., Ginny Foster, Eugene Francis, Vishi Garig, The Granary, Shirley Haynes, Paula Hilton, Inez Holger, A.V. Ireland, Edward P. Jackson, Carol Jones, Jacksonville Public Library, Mike and Patty Keck, Kat Kerr, Rhiannon Lee, Marshall Lenne, Marie Chidester Lybrook, Cheryl McDavitt, Bobbi McDermott, Middleburg Museum, Barry Mishkind, Jay and Nancy Moore, *Neighbor to Neighbor*, Panera Bread Orange Park, Cathy Parrott, Jill Pellegrin, Penney Farms Community, Julie Pipho, The River House, Richard Preston, Nancy Quatrano, Jack Rhyne, Carrie Richter, Dr. Sandy Rosenberg, Rotary Club of Green Cove Springs, Rotary Club of Orange Park, Luis and JoAnn Ruiz, Mary Ann de Stefano, Teresa Stepzinski, Cynthia Stone, Ph.D., Edry Rowe Surrency, Tom Swartz, Lamar Thames, Stavros Tofalos, Lee Ann Trumbull, Penina Weltman, Karen Walker, Kathleen Walls and many other community members.

Table of Contents

Introduction

Clay sits quietly on the west bank of the St. Johns River. Compared with neighbors Jacksonville and St. Augustine, Clay attracts relatively little attention, and its stories often go untold.

In 2013, members of Clay County Writers were challenged to collaborate on an anthology. More than a dozen local writers set out to explore people, communities, and events that shaped the character of this area. Drawing on historical documents, interviews, and other materials, each writer unearthed a fresh point of view. Residents responded generously, sharing memories, contacts, and other resources.

Organized in roughly chronological order, these stories span the early 1800s to the present. They offer glimpses of the challenges, conflicts, and commitments of a diverse group of people—people who made a difference in Clay and in the world.

Though the stories belong to the individual writers, in all ways, this anthology has been a community effort.

Clay: The County

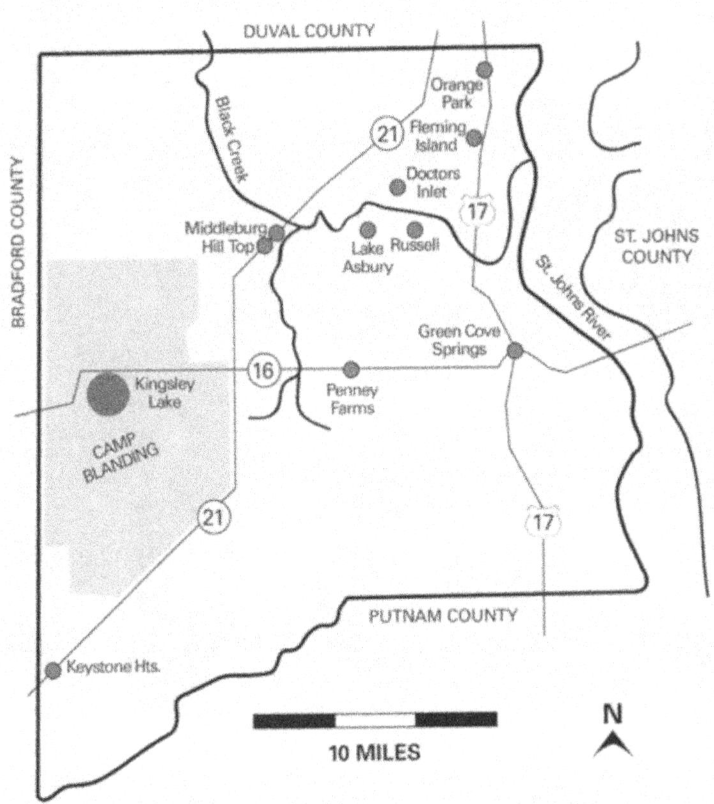

This map shows many locations mentioned in the pages that follow.

Note: Find other Clay County maps at:

http://claycountygov.com/home/showdocument?id=586 (a 2017 map)

http://fcit.usf.edu/florida/maps/galleries/county/clay/index.php (Multiple maps, 1836-2008)

Black Creek with its flora and fauna, from a postcard dated December 25, 1910. In his book Clay County, Kevin Hooper noted that shooting alligators was a "favorite sport" of male tourists visiting from the North. For about $12, they could hire a boat for the purpose in Green Cove Springs or Hibernia. (Courtesy of Clay County Archives.)

Dispatches from a Water Dog: Stories from the Creek

Diane E. Shepard

A creative nonfiction piece told through the eyes of the men and boys working on Black Creek in the 1800s.

A Water Dog's Life

They call me "Water Dog." I work the Creek, work the logs.[1] Pullin' together felled trees, drillin' holes in 'em with my auger and bit, joinin' the logs to fashion rafts.[2] Mindin' my balance, I work the bit and turn the auger while standin' on the log in the water.[3] All the while, ever-vigilant am I for water moccasins and diamondback rattlers who love this Creek and its woods as much as I do.[4] This Creek—Black Creek—as black as ink and deep as night, deep dark waters full of wonder and mystery, deep dark waters so full of history.

---

[1] Arch Fredric Blakey, with an update by Bonita Thomas Deaton, *Parade of Memories, A History of Clay County, Florida*, (Green Cove Springs: Board of Clay County Commissioners, 1995), 123.

[2] Mary Jo McTammany, "When They Said 'The Good Lord Willing,' They Really Meant It," *Clay County Line,* June 7, 2000.

[3] Blakey, *Parade of Memories*, 120-21.

[4] McTammany, "When They Said."

I've got some stories to tell. Just the other day, the boss and me saw an old gator that musta been damn near 18 feet long.[5]

There's a trick to fellin' and cuttin' those tall, gangly pine trees so they fall just right, where we can chain 'em to the cart's underside and haul 'em to the Creek with greater ease.[6]

I work for Thompson and Hart—$1.50 a day, plus bunk and grub.[7] The work is hard, but I don't mind. Besides, Ma always said, hard work builds character. My character must be mighty strong by now.

Before I was old enough to be on the water, to work in and along the Creek, as soon as my chores were done, I used to tear off after my Pa and climb to the top of the old, sturdy oak where Spanish moss hung so low you could almost touch it from the ferry. The oak's spiny limbs reached out over that black water like a ghostly specter. I'd perch up there, almost hangin', my legs wrapped around its branches, wound tight like a coiled rattler. I would stretch as far as I could for a glimpse of someone movin' cattle across Black Creek, or a boat or ferry comin' around the bend. Other times, if I was really lucky, I would see Pa. He'd be workin' the logs, or sometimes, he was slingin' bags of cotton, corn, or cane onto a waitin' schooner. I would say to myself, I'm gonna do that someday. Now I do.

It's a mighty fine thing to do hard work and see it appreciated in a goodly fashion.

Life here on the Creek can be hard, but we have our fun too. The trick is mixin' the necessaries with the fun. House-raisin's, barn-raisin's, log-rollin's, corn shuckin's, quiltin' bees,

---

[5] Ibid.

[6] Ibid.

[7] Blakey, *Parade of Memories*, 122.

and rail splittin's. We have us some fine dancin' and music and eatin' after.[8]

Secrets of the Creek

Pa says if you get to know a place real well, so well you can find your way around it even in the dark, it will tell you its stories. And, if you're really lucky, it will give up its secrets to you.

Sometimes, I think, you can just see things better in the dark. There's something about the absence of light that lets you see your way clear to what might otherwise have been muddled before.

Got no use for church or preachers, whether they stand at a pulpit or come riding in on a horse.

This land is my altar. This Creek, my church. As black as ink and deep as night. She brings me to a peaceful mind. She is my cathedral, my sacred place, my light.

As soon as my oar hits the water, my spirit is born anew. Being on the Creek is as natural to me as breathing. Pa calls me Water Dog. For as long as I can remember, I have been drawn to this place. It is in my bones.

My boss jokes that I have Creek water coursing through my veins. I reckon he could be right.

Ma says there are places—big cities mostly—where at night, the music comes spillin' out the windows and out the doors, onto the streets, and people take to dancin' and carryin'

[8] Edna McDonald, "The History of Middleburg," *Clay County Leader*, June 30-July 6, 1999, 11.

on, not caring who is watchin' and what they see. But that's not for me.

My music is the music of the Creek. It comes alive at night and makes its own harmony.

When the moon hangs low in the sky, crickets and cicadas, frogs and owls, even gators, make a music all their own. The way the wind moves through the trees—now that's music to me. The wind sounds completely different blowin' through pine needles than it does blowin' through leaves.

Spanish moss hangs from oak canopies far above our heads—swingin' in the breeze like an old woman's hair or a Spaniard's wiry beard. Along the banks of the creek and in the trees in town, it's everywhere.

Ma told me once about a Spanish explorer, Gorez Goz.[9] He bought himself a beautiful Indian squaw, but she had no love for him and wanted to be free. She ran from him and climbed a tree, then dove into the water. He had followed her into the tree, but in his haste to reach her, his long grey beard got tangled up in the limbs and he perished there. As legend has it, his beard continued to grow and spread throughout the trees. And that's how Spanish moss came to be.[10]

---

[9] Postcard from the author's collection.
[10] Ibid.

As Black as Ink and as Deep as Night

I stood watchin', with my hat to my heart, as the ferry brought the bell up the creek for the Methodist Church. Its first tolling was in memory of one of the Branning boys.[11]

Sure, the Creek has claimed some lives in its storied history, but she's saved some too. Take Wash Branning, our mail carrier. As soon as the Union troops arrived, they had it in for poor Wash—said he was a damned spy. They were set to shoot him dead right there on the spot. Well, they gave him a few minutes to pray. He saw his opportunity. Lickety-split, he dove into the Creek and swam underwater a ways. They just kept a-shootin', but couldn't see him on account of the dark water, so they figured he had drowned. They were wrong. A few days later, he showed up at the Dillaberrys' wet, hungry, and smellin' like the Creek. Lucky devil.[12]

They call me Water Dog. I work the Creek. I work the logs. Over the years, I've seen much on this Creek and some of its stories I've shared with you. But the deepest secrets of the Creek, I keep. Just like with courtin' a lady, her best secrets are safe with me.

If you get to know a place real well, so well you can find your way around it even in the dark, it will get inside you and never let you go. It will tell you its stories. And, if you're really lucky, it will give up its secrets to you.

Black Creek is that place for me.

---

[11] Blakey, *Parade of Memories*, 56.
[12] Ibid, 87.

Remember Me

Diane E. Shepard

As this War rages on,
more time passes,
harder it is to remember
what it was like before
this dreadful War invaded our lives.

I keep a lock of his dark hair
tucked inside my locket,
pressed forget-me-nots he gave me
safe inside my apron pocket.

I try real hard to remember him,
his face, his eyes, the dimple in his chin,
our sweet life together.
Memories of our boys and our men
each passing day grows ever dim.

Their voices echo in our ears
as they whisper through our tears,
Remember me.
How hard we try.
For if you do,
we will not die.

Embedded in Clay

We cannot lose hope. It is the
guiding light that we live by.
Word came late on a September afternoon.
A basket of white linens, freshly washed,
in my hands.
Lightning scarred the darkening sky,
thunder's drum beat in the distance.

I saw them coming across the field,
in step with thunder's din.
My heart closed—shut tight right then.

Last night, I heard the owl call my beloved's
name. I didn't need to hear their words.
Dropping to my knees, the clean white
linens falling to the dirt,
his last words to me
ringing in my ears,
Remember me.

The historic Clark-Chalker House in Middleburg in 1988, where Martha Bardin Chalker lived much of her life. (Courtesy of the State Archives of Florida.)

Woman of the Creek

Diane E. Shepard

In the early 1930s, when Martha Chalker was in her late 80s, she and other longtime residents were interviewed for a short article about Middleburg. Martha lived on Black Creek nearly all her life and was generally regarded as a matriarch of the community. I became captivated by her and her obvious spirit and fortitude. This creative nonfiction piece is my tribute to her: as child, as woman, as matriarch.

Life is made up of stories—those of the memory, those spun from the heart, and those that are just simply true. Come sit with me on my porch for a spell, and I will tell you a few.

The Creek Calls to Me—Freedom Song

It might as well have been an ocean, as deep and dark as it was to me. This Creek, jet black as Papa's hair and deeper than I cared to be.

I remember sitting on its banks. Weaving daisy chains from weeds, I even fashioned little boats from twisted twigs and leaves. Setting them to drift in the Creek, I watched them longingly, a feeling I could not name shot through me. I had set them free—why could it not be me? But this was before I realized the Creek was calling me. This was before I realized the Creek had set me free.

Father used to say that I roamed like a wily panther all over Black Creek and this land. "I walked all over it in no time."[13]

I left my father's care when I was still a young girl and came to Hoyt House at the center of town.[14]

There I learned all the things a 'proper' lady should know. But when no one was paying me any mind, I ran to the Creek and played along its banks—just like the boys did. After lessons, I'd kick off my shoes and dart like a rabbit along the winding paths, pulling red satin ribbons out of my hair as I ran, flinging them hither and yon. I still remember looking back to watch them sail down to the ground—little banners of freedom. My hair, now as unrestricted as the rest of me, flew every which way.

My bare feet met the ground. I sunk my toes into the cool, dark earth and wiggled them like burrowing earthworms. I reveled in my escape from duty. But like anything truly good, it did not last.

Faeries, Fireflies, and Fate

I grew up near the remains of Fort Heilman; disease and death seemed always at our doorstep.

I remember stories, like a faraway, smoky dream, of makeshift huts and tents dotting the grounds around the fort and up and down the streets. They seemed to spring up overnight like wild mushrooms, as yet another family took refuge within their

---

[13] Francis A. Ewell, "The Story of Middleburg," (paper presented at a meeting of the Jacksonville Historical Society, c. 1932).

[14] Mary Jo McTammany, "From Girl to Woman in Black Creek," *Clay County Line,* Sept. 22, 2004, 2.

faerie rings, there amongst the masses, fearing, as we all did, Indian muskets and hatchets.[15]

At night, my head full of Grimm's faerie tales, I dreamt of gypsies, princesses, and soldiers 'round a campfire, sleeping inside mushroom tents. Their lives as transitory and fleeting as fireflies—flying, living, lighting, breathing, then suddenly, their light extinguished.

Sometimes, when the wind came off the Creek just right, the smell of smoke or the stench of Death moved down the street, reached in through open windows while we slept. Sometimes it lingered, hung in the air like a thick, dark fog you cannot see. On those days, in particular, we hurried through town to get our errands done looking like bandits with handkerchiefs (mine dotted with purple violets) held to our faces.

But we had our fun and frivolity too. Some nights camping like gypsies by moonlight: we cooked our food, and sang, and danced by the fire.[16] We practiced the 'Chivari' tradition whenever anyone got married—banging pots and pans together and ringing bells in a noisy mock 'serenade' for the newlyweds. Only a sampling of the wedding cake could quiet our clamor.[17]

When I was 14, our plantation doubled in size. Father purchased the fine rambling house on Main Street that had been my school.[18]

When I was 20, I married my sweetheart in the parlor of that same house, and it became my own home. This is where I have lived all my life.[19]

---

[15] McTammany, "From Girl to Woman."
[16] Ewell, "The Story of Middleburg," 8.
[17] Blakey, *Parade of Memories*, 132.
[18] McTammany, 2.

During the Great War, my sweetheart Albert and I exchanged letters. He wrote bits of poetry for me full of sweet talk and finery.[20] "I didn't know what it was to love or how much I loved you until now."[21]

One evening during the War, my curiosity was nearly the death of me. Two thousand colored troops were quartered here. Federal officers dined right here at Clark House. As the troops marched by out in front, I ran out onto the gallery, and watched with horrified fascination. Just then, a Negro private shot at a goose running in our yard, and I was nearly grazed by the bullet.[22]

"Since I was so reckless, he came near getting one, [a silly goose], anyhow."[23] I can laugh about it now.

I remember the terrible noise during the Battle of Tiger Head. My colored maid hid under the bed all day.[24]

My Albert set up the first private ferry after the War. The commissioners set his rates: The one-way passage for a person was 10 cents, or for a horse and buggy, 50 cents.[25]

I had many children—that was the way back then.[26]

---

[19] Ibid.

[20] Albert S. Chalker, Martha Bardin Chalker, Letters, 1864-1865 http://worldcat.org/title/letters-1864-1865/oclc/32413780. See also Tracy J. Revels, *Grander in Her Daughters: Florida's Women During the Civil War*, (Columbia: University of South Carolina Press, 2004), 40.

[21] Ibid., Revels.

[22] Ewell, "The Story of Middleburg."

[23] Ibid.

[24] Ibid.

[25] Blakey, Parade of Memories, 134.

[26] "United States Census, 1880," Index and Images, FamilySearch http://familysearch.org/pal:/MM9.1.1/MNZM-HBD; "United States Census, 1900," http://familysearch.org/pa;:/MM9.1.1/M3DR-ZTS.

The mail was our lifeblood then, still is. It used to come by steamboat once a week. But that was long ago. My Albert operated the post office for a time. He would deliver people their mail over the counter from this very house.[27]

My son George took it over and ran it out of his store on Main Street for many years.[28]

After Albert passed, I took in boarders to make ends meet. I still had daughters at home, but they were older then.[29] They did right fine for themselves. All my children did.

Full of Life

No, I was no world traveler. I've lived here all my life. I raised my family here, and this is where I will die.[30] Some would call my window on the world too narrow, too small. But how do you truly measure a life? By how wide one sees? What places they've been, or how many lives they have touched?

I have seen a good many things in my nearly 90 years. I buried my parents, my siblings, my husband. I've had to watch too many of my children be lowered into the earth.[31] Something no mother should ever have to do.

---

[27] "Picturesque Middleburg." *Florida Times-Union,* December 10, 1937; "Middleburg United Methodist Cemetery, Middleburg, Clay County, Fla.," http://files.usgwarchives.net/fl/clay/cemetery/middleburg.txt.

[28] "First Post Master in Middleburg Dates Back to 1832," *The Middleburg Press,* Nov. 17, 1988, 12.

[29] United States Census, 1900.

[30] "Florida Deaths, 1877-1939," Index, FamilySearch http://familysearch.org/pal:MM9.1.1/FPCT-Martha Ann Chalker, Feb. 3, 1936, citing Middleburg, Clay, Florida, reference cn2406; FHL microfilm 2135878.

[31] Ibid.

When things got hard here, many fled, but I remained. Sure, things were tough, but that which you cannot overcome, you simply must endure.

It's all in the soundness of the structure—the way in which a bird builds his nest—that determines how well it can weather a storm. Well, my house is strong and sturdy. So am I. I have weathered well my losses and I have lived to tell.

My house is made of hand-hewn heart pine, held together with pegs and tongue and groove timber, both inside and out.[32] My home still stands, some 90 years later. As do I. I am rooted to this place, this Creek, this house—my home. Like one of Mother's lace doilies, so tightly knitted am I to this place, so firmly fixed to this landscape, securely woven like the hummingbird nest, I am to this place, my home, this Creek, Black Creek—as deep and dark and full of life. This is where I will die. I could not leave it if I tried.

My life is made up of stories, just whispers of memories, bitter and sweet, and some true.

I've lived on this Creek all my life.

Now my story is history to you.

---

[32] "A Brief Summary of Middleburg History," *Clay Countian*, March 15, 1984.

Selected References

Blakey, Arch Fredric, with an update by Bonita Thomas Deaton. *Parade of Memories, A History of Clay County, Florida.* Clay County: Board of County Commissioners, 1995.

Chalker, Albert S. Chalker and Martha Bardin Chalker, "Letters, 1864-1865." http://worldcat.org/title/letters-1864-1865/oclc/32413780.

Revels, Tracy J. *Grander in Her Daughters: Florida's Women During the Civil Wa*r. Columbia: University of South Carolina Press, 2004.

Fishing along Black Creek. In addition to providing food and enabling river transportation of supplies, livestock, and people, the lumber and turpentine industries also depended on the Creek. (Courtesy of Clay County Archives.)

Brothers Procession

Major Bryan J. Pitchford

They gather in the early morning mists
before the sun crests the horizon.
Blue Soldiers in blue uniforms,
brown warriors in native skins,
freedom fighters with timeless causes,
all Patriots in their own rights.

They gather, assembling for morning
muster, calling out each name three times
then a service number.
Three shots from seven rifles in sequence,
twenty-one-gun salutes.

They gather along the shore.
Marching out in rank and file
along A Avenue in sight of
Kingsley Lake, round as a silver dollar.
The avant-garde bearing a tattered guidon [33]
calling cadence from the afterlife,
haunting baritones, solemn and slow.
One last gathering before
they pass on to the next world.

---

[33] A guidon refers to a small flag or pennant often used to designate a military unit.

Ghostly faces, disembodied voices
trailing across the lake at dawn.
Whispering up into the heavens,
eternal secrets and regrets.

From Starke through Middleburg they gather,
through Orange Park and Jacksonville
to the pier. From the old fort to the port,
by way of forgotten boulevards between the
trees. They follow the Saint Johns River,
the old supply route, to the final call.

Marching through the afternoon,
a silent parade without spectators.
By dusk they have disappeared.
Returned to the port they wait for their ship.
Bringing a promise of final peace.
"Charon's Dream" to the Grey Havens
beyond the River Styx.

Every night they fade away and
every morning they are born again.
Phoenix, the warrior's spirit,
they awake to gather.[34]

---

[34] Inspiration for this poem came in the form of a military art book by Renée Klish, *Art of the American Soldier: Documenting Military History Through Artists' Eyes and in Their Own Words*. (Washington, D.C.: Center of Military History, 2011).

A postcard showing infantry troops training at Camp Blanding during the early 1940s, from photos taken by the U.S. Army Signal Corps. As the images show, recruits initially learned on equipment left over from World War I. (Courtesy of Clay County Archives.)

Pvt. Robert C. Burns

Major Bryan J. Pitchford

Private Robert C. Burns,
Bob or Robby to his friends,
raised in Middleburg, from age three,
the only local boy in our company.

Robby was like any other young recruit.
He knew he was immortal, though
not in the traditional sense,
all bravery, charging through bullets
and explosions into battle.

He dreamed of a different immortality,
eternity through words and pictures.
Robby joined the Army a gentle soul,
a painter, poet, warrior artist.

He came to Camp Blanding fresh,
naïve. Robby loved the Army,
though it disagreed with him at times.
He often said it stifled his creativity
and suffocated his free spirit.

Embedded in Clay

Our poor wooden barracks looked
Like a concentration camp,
sterile buildings in a perfect grid.
Upended Coca-Cola bottles
buried in the dirt, round bottoms
glowing in the moonlight.
Reflective walkways.

Robby knew the land and would
lead our squad off into the woods,
compass needles lit by the white moon.
Our own Dead Poets Society of
actors, painters, and poets.

Sometimes Robby chronicled our training in
paintings, abstract acrylics, and watercolors.
Other times his reports consisted of lengthy
narratives, stanzas thick with figurative language.
Reporting on the war in sonnets and
sestinas, silent witness to the war.

Burns saw the world with a paintbrush,
painting with his heart and blood.
He loved enough paintings,
read enough poetry.
He spoke in Psalms and Proverbs.

Only one painting survives.
Not his most famous, or
even most ambitious work.
A humble painting,
honest and simple
like Burns himself.
A typical scene,
"Troop Movement," 1942.[35]

[35] Informed by this book by Robert Hawk, *Florida's Army: Militia/State Troops/National Guard 1565-1985*. (Englewood, Fla.: Pineapple Press, Inc., 1986).

Artist's interpretation of the Laurel Grove Plantation. Zephaniah Kingsley, Jr. purchased the property in 1803 and further developed the land. The Kingsleys grew Sea Island cotton, potatoes, peas, and beans, as well as hundreds of orange trees. This image by Nancy Freeman depicts Laurel Grove as she imagined it in 1812. (Courtesy of Clay County Archives.)

Women Forming Clay

Joan T. Warren

History lessons tend to immortalize prominent men—businessmen, military officers, politicians—while stories of women often go untold. Such is the case in Clay County. In Orange Park, for example, Kingsley Avenue is named for plantation owner Zephaniah Kingsley, Jr. Fleming Island reflects Spanish land grant holder Colonel Lewis Fleming. In Green Cove Springs, Borden's Dairy Products was named for the family of John Gail Borden. We hear less about the courageous women with these surnames who, through self-sacrifice and dedication, helped form Clay County's character. Their contributions can inspire us to make a positive difference in our communities.

Spanish Florida: Anna Kingsley

On a hot summer day in 1806, a merchant's boat rowed along the St. Johns River. As the boat approached the banks, cypress knees could be seen dotting the river's edge. Delicate fringes of moss swayed from the fern-laden branches of ancient oaks, and wild grape vines knit trees to bushes. A snake dropped from a branch to the water. A plantation along the river's edge offered a refreshing, orange-blossom breeze, carrying with it the low hum of singing from the fields. Slave trader, merchant, and plantation owner Zephaniah Kingsley, Jr. returned from Havana, Cuba, his ship laden with supplies for his retail shop, also carried slaves to work in his fields, and his new wife, Anna.

Anna was a teen, tall and slender, a stately beauty. Their child, conceived in transit, grew within her.[36] She surveyed her new home, a vast and beautiful plantation with orange groves and fields of cotton, corn, beans, and potatoes.[37] A two-story house stood by the river. Beyond this were rows of smaller houses, each with its own small garden,[38] for the slaves who made all this possible.[39]

At the time, slavery was common in Africa, but Anna was born an African princess named Anta Majigeen Ndiaye. Raiders from warring tribes stole her away in the night and sold her to slave traders.[40] Anna survived captivity on Gorée Island, Africa, an inhumane holding site, then traveled in putrid conditions in a slave-trading ship to Havana. From princess to slave, she stood on the platform for sale.[41] Zephaniah bought her and made her his wife.

Within five years, Anna and Zephaniah had three children. She managed the plantation during Zephaniah's frequent business trips by sea. Zephaniah officially emancipated Anna and their children. From royalty to slavery to freedom, Anna became a slaveholder and landowner herself. By 1812, she built a two-story home across the river with farmland, produce, livestock, and homes for her 12 slaves. She lived with her children, as was customary in her homeland, where royal wives

---

[36] Daniel L. Schafer, *Anna Madgigine Jai Kingsley: African Princess, Florida Slave, Plantation Slaveowner,* (Gainesville: University Press of Florida, 2010), 27.
[37] Ibid., 29.
[38] Ibid.
[39] Daniel L. Schafer, *Zephaniah Kingsley Jr. and the Atlantic World: Slave Trader, Plantation Owner, Emancipator* (Gainesville: University Press of Florida, 2013),73.
[40] Schafer, *Anna Madgigine*, 14.
[41] Ibid., 19, 23.

and their children lived separately from men. Anna continued her spousal relationship with Zephaniah and her work managing Laurel Grove. They treated slaves well and facilitated emancipation for many.[42]

This time of peaceful plantation life under Spanish rule did not last long. Insurgent "Patriots" from the United States rose up against the Spanish government.[43] They captured Zephaniah, took over his plantation as headquarters, and raided Indian villages. The Seminoles, in turn, burned Laurel Grove, yet the main house stood, being fortified with cannons and seven-foot walls.[44]

Some Patriots withdrew back to the States, but others remained, squatted in Laurel Grove, and plundered the surrounding areas for goods and slaves to steal. Anna's family was across the river. If captured, they would be sold into slavery. Realizing this, Anna rowed to a Spanish gunboat to request protection for her family and slaves. She volunteered to lead a team to Laurel Grove to rescue slaves, set the house afire and disable the cannons so rebels could no longer use it as headquarters.

As she returned to the gunboat, her mission complete, the Spanish commander saw no flames. He thought she had deceived him.[45]

"You went to set a fire, and you haven't done anything?"[46] he questioned, disdainfully.

---

[42] Ibid., 32-34.
[43] Rembert W. Patrick, *Florida Fiasco: Rampant Rebels on the Georgia-Florida Frontier, 1810-1815*. (Athens: University of Georgia Press, 1954), quoted in ibid., 39.
[44] Ibid., 40.
[45] Schafer, *Anna Madgigine*, 40-42.
[46] Ibid., 42.

"Wait a moment,"[47] was her confident reply. Then the cannons exploded. The house was ablaze.

Anna did not stop there. She requested an escort to her property, where she loaded up food and weapons. Then she set her own place afire so it could not be used as a center for lawless plundering. The Spanish transported Anna, her children, and her slaves, to Fernandina, where Zephaniah later joined her.[48]

They rebuilt a plantation on nearby Fort George Island, where Anna remained for many years. Then, when statehood created problems for their freedom, the Kingsley family moved to Haiti to establish a free black community. After Zephaniah's death, she returned to defend his will. She founded a small community of free blacks in an area now known as the Arlington section of Jacksonville, Florida. [49] Throughout life, Anna emancipated many slaves and helped them establish their lives in freedom.[50]

Though not long on the fields of Laurel Grove, Anna's intelligence, character, and sacrificial heroism made a lasting impression. Her life influenced her husband's views, as he turned from trading slaves to building free black communities. Anna's work carried seeds of dignity, freedom, and pride to the slaves she freed. Her life inspired respect among people of many nationalities and perspectives, well beyond her time on earth.[51]

---

[47] Ibid.
[48] Ibid., 43-44.
[49] Author's note: that community is now known as Jacksonville's Arlington section.
[50] Ibid., chapters 7-9.
[51] Ibid., 122-128.

Farther along the River: Margaret Seton Fleming

The year 1837 marked the arrival of Colonel Lewis Fleming's second wife, Margaret Seton Fleming, to his plantation, Hibernia, on what is now called Fleming Island. A family friend since childhood, she had helped nurture Lewis' children after the death of his first wife in 1832. Known as kind and hospitable, but also strong, forthright, full of energy and intelligence,[52] Margaret was happy to have finally won Lewis' grieving heart.

Over the next 20-plus years, the Flemings prospered on what would come to be known as Fleming Island. Because the original house was burned in the Seminole war, they lived in a refurbished warehouse at first. Gradually, they rebuilt the Hibernia plantation house as a 32-room white manor with dark-green shutters, wide piazzas, and square pillars. Pink-blossomed crepe myrtle trees lined the path from the dock, and columns of oaks lined a walking path in the back, a perfect setting for the entertaining they so enjoyed.

Together, Margaret and Lewis had seven children, and she took pleasure in caring for and teaching the children around her. She dedicated herself to help and educate slaves and began a Sunday school in her home—open to all. The Flemings' slave families lived in cottages, each with a garden plot on the plantation of over a thousand acres. Their burden of captivity was lifted during the evenings through sharing good food, homespun music, and games.[53,54]

---

[52] Margaret Seton Fleming Biddle, *Hibernia: The Unreturning Tide*. (New York: Vantage Press, 1974), 35, 40.

[53] Ibid., 39-42.

[54] W. J. Stillman, *Autobiography of a Journalist* (London: 1901), quoted in Ibid., 42, 43.

This seemingly idyllic lifestyle met bitter years when death and war visited Hibernia. Margaret's step-son, George, a physician turned reverend, died young from a heart ailment. Her eldest son, Charles, while visiting Chicago said he witnessed a level of abuse and poverty among free Africans that he had never seen in the South. Charles thought the author of Uncle Tom's Cabin, abolitionist Harriet Beecher Stowe, was stirring up ill will that would make life worse for everyone, including slaves.[55] He chose to attend military school and, when the Civil War ensued, became an officer in the Confederate Army.

During the war, supply boats and steamboat travel along the river ceased, doing away with luxuries like coffee, flour, and sugar.[56] Lewis's sons from his first marriage enlisted in the war while still in their teens, and then Lewis also died from heart disease. Margaret, her young daughters, and some of their devoted slaves worked long days and nights to survive. Then, late one evening, Union soldiers confiscated Hibernia Plantation. Margaret and her daughters fled to Ft. Heilman in Middleburg, then on to Lake City. There, Margaret received the disturbing news that her beloved son, Seton, had died in the Battle of Cold Harbour.[57] Though desperately grieving, Margaret still found the strength to nurse wounded soldiers in Lake City, a devoted service she continued through the end of the war.[58]

---

[55] Eugenia Price, *Margaret's Story* (Franklin, Tenn.: Providence House, 2008). Though a work of fiction about a real family, Price documents her research in her accompanying publication, *Diary of a Novel: The Story of Writing Margaret's Story* (New York: Lippincott & Crowell, 1980).
[56] Biddle, *Hibernia*, 46.
[57] "Florida's 'Gone with the Wind,'" Florida Irish Heritage Center, Apr. 15, 2011, a review of Price's book. https://floridairishheritagecenter.wordpress.com/2011/04/15/floridas-gone-with-the-wind/.
[58] Biddle, *Hibernia*, 54.

Afterward, Margaret returned to Hibernia. It lay in shambles. The livestock was gone. The vegetable and fruit fields were barren. Charred remains of fine furnishings and floorboards lay by the fireplace, a casualty of careless soldiers on cold nights. On the second floor, vines grew into the house through broken windows. Sons Frederic, Frank, and William, along with some devoted friends (former slaves) returned to help. Margaret worked tirelessly without complaint or wistful talk of her former life.[59]

Hibernia came to thrive again, this time as a haven for northern guests—a place of respite for many.[60] When Harriet Beecher Stowe (whom Seton blamed for the war, and apparently, President Lincoln did, too)[61] came to visit, Margaret extended grace and befriended Mrs. Stowe.[62]

Several years later, Margaret faced another disheartening loss. Not knowing the deadly nature of yellow fever, she sent her closest daughter, Maggie, to nurse relatives in their illness. Sadly, Maggie also died of yellow fever.[63] Margaret's heartache over this loss darkened her final days. She blamed herself. Within four months, just as her dream for a small Episcopal church at Hibernia was about to be fulfilled, she passed. The first service in the new building was Margaret's funeral.[64]

---

[59] Ibid., 66.

[60] Dr. Bronson, "Hibernia, Clay County, Florida," http://drbronsontours.com/bronsonhibernia.html.

[61] Reports of Lincoln's exact views are often regarded as hearsay, yet in a copy of Stowe's book, *Sunny Memories from Foreign Lands,* available for auction on October 2, 2016 (https://new.liveauctioneers.com/item/748325). Lincoln's signature appeared with this *hand-written inscription,* "Mrs. Stowe, The author of this great war, A. Lincoln Nov. 19, 1863."

[62] Price, Margaret's Story, 497.

[63] Ibid., 508.

[64] Louise Stanton Warren and Leni Bessette, "Flemings' Story Is Story of N. Florida," *Clay County Line*, May 17, 2006, http://jacksonville.com/tu-online/stories/051706/nec_21882079.shtml#.WXJj7emQyUk.

Penelope Borden Hamilton was a founder of the Village Improvement Association (VIA) in Green Cove Springs. Heir to the Borden Dairy fortune, she contributed generously to causes she believed in. She donated land to the VIA at the corner on Palmetto, where its headquarters still stands. (Courtesy of Clay County Archives.)

Margaret's son Francis went on to become governor of Florida in 1889 and created the first State Board of Health to combat yellow fever.[65] Margaret's son Frederic served in the Florida Legislature and reportedly lost an election for tipping his hat to a black man. He donated land to many former slaves and fed all who lived near Hibernia.[66] The inn operated many more years under her children's management. Margaret's life of faith, love, hospitality, and service paved the way for future generations to adapt to challenges, labor without complaint and embrace those with differing viewpoints.

An Era of Improvements: Penelope Borden Hamilton

At the turn of the twentieth century, Green Cove Springs was a popular tourist destination known for its cleanliness, boardwalks, and gardens. Such amenities were due to the efforts of a group of women—the Village Improvement Association (VIA)—and one of its most active members: Penelope Borden.

Penelope, nicknamed Nellie, was the daughter of John Gail Borden of Borden's Dairy Products, whose father founded Borden's Condensed Milk and built a vast dairy empire.[67] Nellie grew up spending winters in Green Cove Springs and summers in New York. As a teen, she joined her mother and others to form the Village Improvement Association. The VIA held barbecues to raise funds to pay for workers to clean streets, maintain flower beds and construct a boardwalk, which helped keep tourists' shoes and dresses clean. The group installed painted barrels as

---

[65] "Francis P. Fleming," Wikipedia, https://en.wikipedia.org/wiki/Francis_P._Fleming.
[66] Warren and Bessette, "Flemings' Story."
[67] Jim Robison, "Green Cove Springs Brought River Visitors, Not Fabled Youth," *Orlando Sentinel*, April 18, 1993. http://articles.orlandosentinel.com/1993-04-18/news/9304160379_1_cove-springs-green-cove-fountain-of-youth.

trash cans and adorned them with witty sayings to prod folks into using them, such as:

> I am all mouth and vacuum:
> I never get enough,
> So cram me full of orange peel,
> Old papers, trash, and stuff.[68]

Their barrel creations gained international fame, and the emperor of Germany gave them credit for the idea when he borrowed it for his country.[69] Penelope, as leader of the VIA, worked at length to change livestock laws to keep cattle off the streets; she also advocated for the VIA to begin and run the first county library and the town kindergarten.[70]

Nellie was the first president of the Federation of Women's Clubs of the State of Florida.[71] The Federation began in Green Cove Springs as a meeting of five Florida women's clubs. Though women could not vote then, this group shaped change by writing letters, educating the public, and influencing their husbands' votes. Nellie worked tirelessly for the passage of legislation on child labor, fire protection for schools, and

---

[68] "Village Improvement Association, *Women's Club,*" 2011, http://archives.clayclerk.com/markers.html.

[69] Mary Jo McTammany, "In Clay, Women Stepped Forward: Green Cove Group Cleaned Up the Town." *The County Line*, March 26, 2003. http://jacksonville.com/tu-online/stories/032603/nec_12095101.shtml#.WXpIw-mQyUk.

[70] "Village Improvement Association."

[71] Visit Florida Staff, "The Florida Women's Club Movement," Visit Florida, http://visitflorida.com/en-us/articles/2011/september/1890-the-florida-womens-club-movement.html.

compulsory education. The group also assisted Seminole Indians and families in financial need.[72]

Penelope Borden Hamilton donated property for the VIA,[73] as well as land which became the Historic Triangle, including Clay County Archives, Clay County Historic Courthouse and the old Clay County Jail and Historical Museum. While a woman of Nellie's means could have opted for a life of ease, she chose to make a positive difference in the world.

Notable History

These three women—Anna Kingsley, Margaret Seton Fleming, and Penelope Borden Hamilton—along with other dedicated women whose stories remain to be told—are important to the history of Clay County, Florida. Anna, an African princess, sold as a slave, overcame adversity with dignity and courage, then set others free. Margaret dedicated her life to educating children without regard to race or status, persevering with self-sacrifice and hard work after many personal losses. She extended grace to Northerner visitors after the Civil War and left a legacy of faith and hospitality in what is now Fleming Island. Penelope personified civic duty and generosity. In addition to volunteering countless hours to better the community and to educate and protect children, she was instrumental in beginning both the Village Improvement Association and the Federation of Women's Clubs of the State of Florida. In Green Cove Springs, Clay's county seat, the property she donated still serves our community today.

---

[72] A.J. Schenkman, "A Forgotten Borden: Penelope Borden." May 20, 2014. http://blogs.hudsonvalley.com/hudson-valley-history/2014/05/20/a-forgotten-borden-penelope-borden/.

[73] "Village Improvement Association."

The dedication of these and other women in this area laid a foundation for Clay County to become a vibrant, healthy, and caring community. Their strength of character stands as a testament to the significance of women in history. Reaching out to help others, they demonstrated the power of their generosity of spirit.

Selected References

Biddle, Margaret Seton Fleming. *Hibernia: The Unreturning Tide*. New York: Vantage Press, 1974.

Schafer, Daniel L. Anna Madgigine Jai Kingsley: *African Princess, Florida Slave, Plantation Slaveowner*. Gainesville: University Press of Florida, 2010.

__________. Zephaniah Kingsley Jr. and the Atlantic World: *Slave Trader, Plantation Owner, Emancipator*. Gainesville: University Press of Florida, 2013.

This small bust, a newly discovered sculpture by Augusta Fells Savage, was dedicated in 2017 and is now on permanent display at the Jacksonville Public Library's Main Branch. (Courtesy of City of Jacksonville, Jacksonville Public Library.)

Shaping Clay: The Story of Augusta Fells Savage

Paula R. Hilton

Discovering Clay

There was no money for toys, but young Augusta never complained. With 13 brothers and sisters, she learned to make do. And what she did have, in her own back yard in Green Cove Springs, Florida, was clay. Beautiful clay. During a dry spell, it was the shade of the rusty spokes on the bike all her older brothers and sisters shared. Augusta worried it would be hopelessly broken by the time she was big enough to ride it. But after a good storm, the clay became her favorite shade—a deep, vibrant red-orange that reminded her of the last rays of the sun she watched set from her open bedroom window, while she daydreamed about what creatures she would sculpt the next day, whenever she got a break from school and chores.

From as early as Augusta could remember, whenever she held a lump of that gooey clay in her hands, her fingers knew just what to do with it. "At the mud pie age, I began to make 'things' instead of mud pies," she said.[74] In these early years, long before she became one of the most important artists of the Harlem Renaissance, she shaped her clay into tiny ducks, cows, pigs, and chickens. Sometimes she created small people to play with

[74] Theresa Leininger-Miller, *New Negro Artists in Paris: African American Painters and Sculptors in the City of Light, 1922-1934* (Rutgers University Press, 2001), 163.

instead of dolls. She loved these toys more than she could have ever loved store-bought ones, because she had patiently molded each one herself from nothing but the rich earth she scooped up and mixed with water until its consistency was perfect for sculpting.

Augusta's artwork charmed her mother, Cornelia. She was pleased to see her "Gussie's" generous nature on display when she got into the habit of taking requests for sculptures from her siblings and friends and giving them away as gifts. But no matter how hard she tried, nothing Cornelia said could convince her husband that their daughter's ever-growing passion to create was worth encouraging. In fact, Augusta's father, Edward Fells, a Methodist minister who supported his struggling family as a house painter, so disapproved of her sculpting that he once crushed one of her pieces beneath the heel of his boot. In a 1935 interview, Augusta said her father "licked me four or five times a week and almost whipped all the art out of me."[75]

Despite his fierce insistence, Augusta refused to believe Edward when he denounced her beloved clay creatures as "graven images" and said she broke the second commandment each time she made one.[76] Even after he demanded she quit, Augusta continued crafting the animals and people she saw hidden inside the clay, making them come to life in her hands. Instead, she began skipping school to visit the Clay County Steam Brick Company, located about one-fourth mile north of Black Creek and two miles below Middleburg.[77] The clay pit she discovered at the brick company delighted her.

---

[75] "Augusta Savage," http://americanart.si.edu/collections/search/artist/?id=4269.

[76] Leininger-Miller, *New Negro Artists*, 164.

[77] "History of Brick Usage in N.E. Florida." Clay County Archives.

According to Clay County historian, Mary Jo McTammany, the young and curious Augusta found it an abundant source for clay:

> She badgered workmen with questions and was constantly chased away from peering into the drying tunnels or slipping too close to the furnaces. They bribed her with buckets of the rosy moist mixture to make her leave.[78]

But of course, after securing this prized clay, Augusta returned often, "recently acquired bucket in hand, for another payoff."[79]

Spending her school days at the brickyard also gave her a place to escape from Edward's critical eye. Even if she had wanted to obey her father, Augusta would never have abandoned sculpting. Although she was the seventh of 14 children, a desperately poor African-American girl born in the Deep South in 1892, she refused to give up. Everything inside of Augusta screamed that she was meant for more.

---

[78] Mary Jo McTammany, "Artist's Destiny Was Bitter and Sweet," *Florida Times-Union,* Feb. 24, 1999.
[79] Ibid.

Born in Green Cove Springs February 29, 1892, the seventh of 14 children, she was named Augusta Christine Fells. Undated photo. (Courtesy of Clay County Archives.)

Leaving Clay

In 1915, Edward found a new church position in West Palm Beach, Florida. With this move, Augusta's life began to improve. Her talent was undeniable, and the principal of the local school took note, offering her a dollar a day to teach modeling classes to the other students.[80] When Edward Fells realized his daughter could earn money with her art, he stopped condemning her for making it. During this period, Augusta also gained her father's respect by creating an 18-inch sculpture of the Virgin Mary, an image he could find no fault with and even praised. Now that she no longer had to hide to make her art, Augusta could, at last, pursue her passion beyond the confines of her family home.[81]

In 1919, in a quest to earn more income and gain exposure, she persuaded the superintendent of the West Palm Beach County Fair, George Currie, to give her a booth to sell her sculptures. Impressed by Augusta's skill and ambition, Currie became one of her biggest supporters. But not everyone welcomed the young artist to the fair that year. Characteristically unfazed by fair officials who first objected to "a black woman having her own booth," Augusta's work, and her creative display, eventually won them over.[82] She priced her animal sculptures from twenty-five cents to five dollars and enjoyed having one of the most visited booths in the county that year, making over $150, the most money she had ever known. In addition to the profits from her art, she was awarded a $25 prize for "the most original exhibit."[83]

---

[80] Augusta Christine Savage," *Encyclopedia of World Biography*, (Detroit: Gale Research, 1998).
[81] Ibid.
[82] Ibid.
[83] Ibid.

The New York Years

When the excitement of her success at the fair had ended, George Currie did not forget Augusta. Believing her talent deserved support and instruction, he helped her make connections in New York that led to her 1921 admittance to the Cooper Union School of Art, a prestigious public institution in Manhattan that offered her free tuition. Although it was a four-year program, Augusta's instructors waived many of her courses due to how advanced she proved to be upon arrival. She completed the program in just three years. During her time at the Cooper Union, the New York Public Library commissioned Augusta to create a bust of civil rights activist and co-founder of the National Association for the Advancement of Colored People, W. E. B. Du Bois. This important project marked the beginning of Augusta's career as a working artist.[84]

Civil Rights Activism

In 1922, Augusta pursued her dream to study in France, applying to a summer art school program for American women at the palace of Fontainebleau, outside Paris. Although she was among the 100 women personally invited to send an application to the renowned program, the selection committee yielded to pressure from two Alabama women who objected to the idea of traveling with a "colored girl." [85] After receiving these complaints, the committee rejected Augusta's application.

In the face of this injustice, an outraged Augusta chose to fight, becoming "the first black artist to challenge the white art

[84] Henry Louis Gates, Jr. and Evelyn Brooks Higginbotham, "Augusta Savage," in *African American Lives* (Oxford: Oxford University Press, 2004), 746.
[85] Ibid.

establishment openly."[86] Both the African-American and the white press reported on the story. The May 20, 1923, edition of the *New York World* quoted her as saying, "Democracy is a strange thing. My brother was good enough to be accepted in one of the regiments that saw service in France during the war, but it seems his sister is not good enough to be a guest of the country for which he fought."[87]

Although the denial of her application became a city-wide scandal, the committee refused to revoke its decision.[88] And while her courage in exposing the program's racism earned her respect as a civil rights leader, she was labeled a "troublemaker" within the art world from this point forward. "No one knows how many times she was excluded from exhibits, galleries, and museums because of this confrontation," said Romare Bearden, a fellow artist and former student of Augusta, famous for depicting images of African-American life.[89]

A Welcome Change of Luck

If the recipe for luck is truly preparation plus opportunity, then Augusta had been preparing to be lucky since she began making her backyard sculptures in Green Cove Springs. Although she had molded countless pieces in her short lifetime, a life-sized bronze bust of an adolescent boy that she titled *Gamin* (French for "street urchin") became her biggest success and is considered by many to be her finest work. *Opportunity* magazine featured a photograph of *Gamin* on its June 1929 cover to an enthusiastic response that led to two consecutive Julius Rosenwald Fund

---

[86] Ibid, 746-747.
[87] Ibid, 747.
[88] "Augusta Savage," http://dos.dos.state.fl.us/cultural/programs/florida-artists-hall-of-fame/augusta-savage/.
[89] Gates and Higginbotham, *African American Lives*, 747.

fellowships for study in Paris. While finally achieving her dream to study in Europe, Augusta took courses with prominent sculptors and exhibited at key Parisian salons.[90]

Advocating for Young Talent

Soon after the commercial success of *Gamin*, the Great Depression hit the art world hard. Funding for her projects dried up, and Augusta adapted by pursuing teaching and her passion for supporting other African-American artists. In 1932, she opened the Savage School of Arts, which became New York's largest program of free art classes.[91] At her studio in Harlem, Savage often put her own work aside to teach the ambitious young students who soon discovered her studio, including Jacob Lawrence, Romare Bearden, Gwendolyn Knight, and Norman Lewis. Romare Bearden recalled,

> She sacrificed herself and a lot of her art in trying to help the young artists. She set up—on 142nd Street and later on 135th Street—a kind of studio in storefronts. I would pass by there and would see this woman sculpting and modeling. If she looked out and saw you, she'd beckon to you, 'Come on in.'[92]

---

[90] Ibid.
[91] Ibid.
[92] Eugene L. Francis, "A Light and a Fire," in Augusta Fells Savage Cultural Arts Festival program, Green Cove Springs, Fla. 1992.

Gamin, one of her best-known pieces, was on display at the Augusta Savage Arts and Community Center's Black History Celebration in Green Cove Springs, February 22, 2014. (Photo by Paula Hilton.)

Bearden said Augusta attracted Harlem's gifted children "like a magnet," and what most "astonished and delighted" her students was that a talented artist, "who had studied in Europe, had come back to Harlem and was freely available to them."[93]

Augusta was fiercely proud of the young artists she taught and mentored. In a 1935 interview in *Metropolitan Magazine* she said with great humility,

> I have created nothing really beautiful, really lasting, but if I can inspire one of these youngsters to develop the talent I know they possess, then my monument will be in their work.[94]

In 1936, Franklin D. Roosevelt's Works Progress Administration (WPA) chose Augusta as an assistant supervisor for its Federal Arts Project. (FAP) Within a year, Augusta became the first director of the FAP's Harlem Community Art Center, which attracted three thousand students and ten thousand visitors under her leadership.[95]

---

[93] Ibid.
[94] Smithsonian American Art Museum.
[95] Gates and Higginbotham, *African American Lives*, 747.

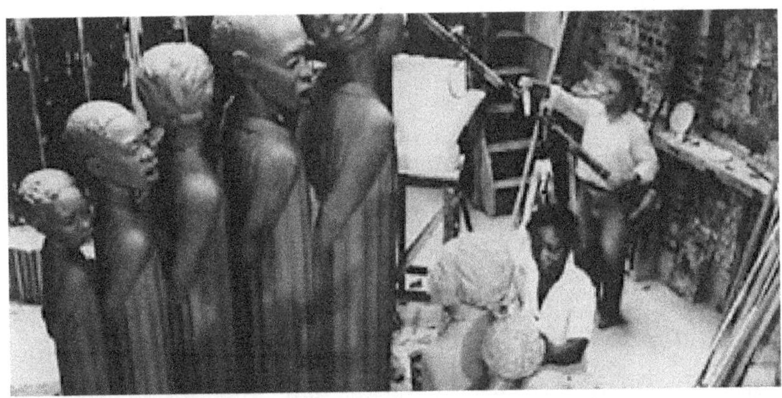

(Two views) Augusta at work on *The Harp*. When organizers of the 1939 World's Fair commissioned her to sculpt a piece that represented the musical contributions of black Americans, her inspiration came from the James Weldon Johnson hymn, *Lift Every Voice and Sing*. (Both views courtesy of Clay County Archives.)

The Harp

In 1938, Augusta took a leave of absence from teaching and administrative work when she was commissioned by the New York World's Fair to sculpt a statue depicting "the American Negro's contribution to music, especially to song." Again, Augusta was a trailblazer, being one of only two African-American artists represented at the fair and one of four women.[96]

Inspired by James Weldon Johnson's song, "Lift Every Voice and Sing," often referred to as "The Black National Anthem," Augusta worked for two years to complete her 16-foot sculpture, which was cast in plaster and "finished to resemble black basalt."[97] It featured a chorus of 12 African-American singers in graduated heights, symbolizing its strings. The sounding board was "formed by the hand and arm of God, and a kneeling man holding music represented the foot pedal." Augusta titled the piece *The Harp*.[98]

That sculpture became one of the most publicized and popular attractions at the 1939 World's Fair. Nonetheless, when the fair ended, it was destroyed when the grounds were razed. There were no facilities to store it, and she didn't have the money to have a work of that magnitude cast in bronze.[99] Augusta was heartbroken.

Later Years

Although Augusta intended to return to her directorial position at the Harlem Community Center after the World's Fair, she discovered Gwendolyn Bennett, a poet and artist she had

---

[96] Ibid.
[97] Smithsonian American Art Museum.
[98] Ibid.
[99] Ibid.

once mentored, had filled her position.[100] Undaunted, Augusta then created and opened the Salon of Contemporary Negro Art in Harlem, "the nation's first gallery devoted to the exhibition and sale of work by African-American artists," but a lack of resources forced it to close only a few months after opening.[101] Augusta continued to create art, and one notable piece she sculpted in 1942, *The Pugilist, New Negro Artists in Paris: African American Painters and Sculptors in the City of Light, 1922-1934*, seems to sum up her spirit. The sculpture of a young African-American man with his head tilted upwards, his arms folded across his chest, has been described as "a confident and defiant figure that appears prepared to take on whatever might come his way."[102]

Savage left city life in 1945, moving to a farm in Saugerties, New York, in the Catskill Mountains. In 1961, failing health made it necessary for her to return to the city. She lived in the Bronx with her daughter, Irene, from her second marriage to carpenter James Savage, until her death from cancer in 1962.[103]

The Birthplace of Hope and Fear

Augusta never forgot her Florida roots. Recalling the home where she won the first of many battles to keep sculpting, she wrote the following poem about Green Cove Springs in 1922:

---

[100] Henry Louis Gates, Jr. and Evelyn Brooks Higginbotham, "Gwendolyn Bennett," in *Harlem Renaissance Lives* (Oxford: Oxford University Press, 2009).
[101] Ibid.
[102] "Augusta Savage—Artist, Civil Rights Activist, Sculptor, Educator," http://biography.com/people/augusta-savage-40495.
[103] Gates and Higginbotham, *Harlem Renaissance.*

The Old Homestead

Augusta Fells Savage

I visited today the old Homestead,
Deserted now for many busy years,
Explored again with memory-laden tread,
The birthplace of so many hopes and fears.

The windlass seemed to creak a doleful tune,
The mocking birds that used to sing so gay
Seem all forgetful of the month of June,
The time to sing their merriest roundelay.

The meadow that to childish eyes did seem
To stretch into the distance mile on mile,
Is but a glen, and now the raging stream,
Is just a little brook that tries to smile.

The brier vines are trailing o'er the ground,
The old red barn will never look the same,
And nothing seemed familiar till I found
The maple bough whereon I carved my name.

It used to stretch far out before the door,
Where through its leaves the sunbeams used to play
And make a dappled shadow on the floor,
Of porches fallen now into decay.

And down my time scarred cheek there crept a tear,
For those who sleep beneath the ocean's foam,
And then a sigh for other hearts so dear,
That rest so gently 'neath the sand of home.

In his reading of the poem, professor of Africana studies Tony Martin, says Augusta balances the nostalgia of remembering her childhood home by confronting "the idealized dream with a less flattering reality—a reality which, nevertheless, still cannot quite dispel the dream of an ancient remembrance."[104]

Legacy in Clay

The community of Green Cove Springs honors Augusta's memory with the Augusta Savage Friendship Park at 321 Walnut Street. Art teacher Cynthia Smith and her students from Charles E. Bennett Elementary plant flowers and clean up the park after school several times a year. Smith, part of the nominating committee for Augusta's induction into the Florida Artists Hall of Fame in 2008, taught her students to mold animals out of clay. Smith said, Augusta:

> started out making little animals, like they are making just down the road. She struggled hard and made it beyond the walls of Green Cove Springs when it was unheard of for a woman to have an art career, let alone a black woman. This is a big deal for Northeast Florida.[105]

As an artist, Smith said Augusta's tenacity inspires her. "Every time something was thrown in her path, she'd work around it." While at Charles E. Bennett, Smith taught her kindergarten through sixth graders that "even though Augusta got

---

[104] Tony Martin, *African Fundamentalism: A Literary and Cultural Anthology of Garvey's Harlem Renaissance* (Dover, Mass.: The Majority Press, 1983), 189.

[105] Mary Maraghy, "Teacher Helps Students Mold Memories of Augusta," *Florida Times-Union*, March 1, 2008.

in trouble for making sculptures, she didn't quit." When asked what excited her students the most about Augusta, Smith said, "they were fascinated she was from Green Cove Springs, just like them."[106]

Another significant way the city of Green Cove Springs remembers Augusta is through The Augusta Savage Arts and Community Center, located near the center of town on the corner of Martin Luther King Jr. Boulevard and Lemon Street, where her family home once stood. It was also the site of the famed Dunbar High School, 1942-1967.[107] Young people gather there to play basketball and baseball and sing in the choir after school. An annual Black History Celebration is held in February at the site. An award-winning dance troupe practices there, aptly named Augusta Savage Power Girls.

"From the time I can first recall the rain falling on the red clay in Florida," Augusta said, "I wanted to make things."[108] From Augusta's early beginnings of molding her beloved clay ducks and chickens out of the Florida mud to the artistic achievements of *Gamin*, *The Pugilist*, and *The Harp*—sculptor, educator, and civil rights activist, Augusta Fells Savage grew up to be one of the greatest artists of the Harlem Renaissance. Her lifelong fight against racism, sexism, and poverty—and her refusal to be daunted by any of these obstacles—makes her one of Florida's most notable people.

---

[106] Interview with Cynthia Smith, Aug. 2, 2016.

[107] Kenneth Detwyler Jr. "Dunbar High School, A Look Back," *Clay Today,* June 22, 2016. http://claytodayonline.com/stories/dunbar-high-school-a-look-back,2760.

[108] Alan Schroeder, *In Her Hands: The Story of Sculptor Augusta Savage* (New York: Lee & Low Books, 2009).

Augusta Fells Savage Timeline

1892—Born February 29 in Green Cove Springs, Florida.

1915—The Fells family moved to West Palm Beach, Florida.

1919—Entered the West Palm Beach County Fair; won a prize for the most original exhibit.

1921—Admitted to Cooper Union School of Art; finished the four-year program in three years.

1922—Invited to apply to a summer art school program for American women at Fontainebleau Palace outside Paris. Her application was rejected due to complaints about her race. Wrote her poem, "The Old Homestead," about Green Cove Springs.

1923—Openly challenged the white art establishment in an interview with the *New York World.*

1929—*Opportunity* magazine featured *Gamin*, one of her most critically acclaimed sculptures, on its cover. Received a Julius Rosenwald Fund Fellowship to Paris. Augusta finally realized her dream to study art in Europe.

1932—Opened Savage School of Arts, which became New York City's largest free art program.

1936—Augusta was named assistant supervisor for the WPA's Federal Arts Project (FAP).

1937—Named the first director of FAP's Harlem Community Art Center.

1939—At the New York World's Fair, her 16-foot sculpture, *The Harp*, became one of the most popular and critically acclaimed attractions.

1942—Sculpted one of her final pieces to become well-known, *The Pugilist.*

1945—Moved to Saugerties, New York, in the Catskill Mountains.

1962—Died after a long battle with cancer, in the Bronx home of her daughter, Irene.

2008—Inducted into the Florida Artists Hall of Fame.

2017—Jacksonville Public Library unveils a newly discovered work: a small bust by Augusta, unnamed, now displayed in its Main Library art collection. Meanwhile, Green Cove Springs has approved a stand-alone Augusta Savage Festival to be headed up by Eugene Francis.

Selected References

Gates, Henry Louis Jr. and Higginbotham, Evelyn Brooks. "Augusta Savage." In *African-American Lives*. Oxford: Oxford University Press, 2004.

Leininger-Miller, Theresa. *New Negro Artists in Paris: African-American Painters and Sculptors in the City of Light, 1922-1934.* Hempstead, NY: Rutgers University Press, 2001.

Martin, Tony. *African Fundamentalism: A Literary and Cultural Anthology of Garvey's Harlem Renaissance*. New York: The Majority Press, 1983.

Schroeder, Alan. *In Her Hands: The Story of Sculptor Augusta Savage*. New York, NY: Lee & Low Books, 2009.

The Granary health food store has been a local institution since 1979. Built in 1887, the structure served as the Caretaker's Cottage during the days of the primate research center. (Photo by Wanda Glennon Canady.)

Looking for Bokar at Orange Park's Monkey Farm

Tim Gilmore

Find earlier versions of this piece online at jaxpsychogeo.com.

"Humanizing the Ape"

Because of the "Chimcracker Caper," Otto Tinklepaugh was dismissed from the Monkey Farm.[109]

The caper had nothing to do with the Humanzee, nothing to do with escaped monkeys that terrorized the small town of Orange Park at night, and nothing to do with mutant effects from the chimpanzee radiation experiments.

Chimcrackers were not hybrids of chimpanzees and Florida crackers or rednecks. They were preprocessed hardtack biscuits for chimps, and Tinklepaugh's erroneous dietary information led to chimp weight loss.

Throughout the 35 years the Yerkes Laboratories of Primate Biology, which locals referred to as the Monkey Farm, operated in Orange Park, the lab usually kept a low profile.

---

[109] Donald A. Dewsbury, *Monkey Farm: A History of the Yerkes Laboratories of Orange Park, Florida, 1930-1965*, (Lewisburg, Penn.: Bucknell University Press, 2005), 125-128.

When the primate research facility opened in Orange Park in 1930, Yale psychologist Robert Yerkes decided it was best to keep a low profile. He wrote, "It is true we do not court publicity. Far too often it results in misunderstanding, unenlightened criticism or, worse still, ridicule." Sure enough, the operation inspired rumors and tall tales that continue to be repeated to this day. (Courtesy of Clay County Archives.) http://jacksonville.com /community/my_clay_sun/2009-07-03/story/rumors_still_ abound_about_orange_parks_monkey_farm

Kingsley Avenue was still a two-lane road through the woods, and the lab was barely visible in the "blackjack ridge" of oaks and pines. It didn't take long for locals to consider the lab's low visibility as secrecy. Urban legends abounded.

It's true, however, that Donald and Gua were raised together as infants. In 1932, when Gua, the female chimpanzee, was seven-and-a-half-months old, she went to live with 10-month-old Donald, the son of Winthrop and Luella Kellogg.

In their 1933 book, *The Ape and the Child*, the Kelloggs documented Donald's meager influence on Gua's development. Gua would stick out her lips in an effort to say, "Papa," but that was as close as she came to speaking. Donald, meanwhile, sometimes sounded more chimpanzee than human.[110]

"From 7:00 a.m. to 6:30 p.m. the Kelloggs were incessantly occupied with the children, dressing, feeding and cuddling them," *Time* magazine reported June 19, 1933 in an article titled "Babe and Ape."[111]

In nearly every way, Gua learned more quickly and outperformed Donald. She was first to walk upright, and Donald imitated her manner of walking. Gua recognized her reflection before Donald recognized his; she understood pictures in children's books before Donald did; and she taught Donald to bite people and walls. Gua loved to be tickled and sometimes engaged in long sessions of tickling herself.

The Kelloggs' study is one of the most radical "cross-fostering" experiments ever conducted, prodding the distinctions

---

[110] W.N. and L.A. Kellogg, *The Ape and the Child: A Study of Environmental Influence upon Early Behavior* (New York: McGraw-Hill, 1933), 287.

[111] "Babe and Ape," *Time* magazine, http://content.time.com/time/subscriber/article/0,33009,789375,00.html.

between nature and nurture. Environment, they concluded, had the greatest effect on learning other than natural limitations. Though Winthrop Kellogg had first proposed the experiment in a 1931 *Psychological Review* article called "Humanizing the Ape,"[112] Donald seemed to show more signs of simianization than Gua did of humanization.

Robert Yerkes, the Yale psychologist and primatologist who founded the Monkey Farm, also had a great interest in eugenics, the study of improving the genetic quality of human beings through controlled breeding. In 1923, he wrote, "No one of us as a citizen can afford to ignore the menace of race deterioration." At Yale, he chaired the Committee on Inheritance of Mental Traits, a section of Yale's Eugenics Office. Five years after *Time* published "Babe and Ape," the magazine put Adolf Hitler on its cover as "Man of the Year."

Most of Yerkes' studies at the Monkey Farm, however, concerned ape cognition and socialization, operant conditioning, and sexual and family relationships. Sometimes he dressed Judy, his favorite chimp, in pink and drove her around in his car.

The Kelloggs' experiment received notoriety and intense criticism. Most of the lab's work garnered much less attention, which only made North Florida residents more suspicious. In December 2006, the Discovery Channel aired an absurd special about Oliver the Humanzee (rhymes with chimpanzee), in which a psychology professor refers to an unnamed source who supposedly told him that just such a human-chimp hybrid was bred at the Monkey Farm in the 1920s.[113]

---

[112] W.N. Kellogg, "Humanizing the Ape," *Psychological Review*, 38, 2 (March 1931): 160-176.

[113] Charlie Patton, "Rumors Still Abound about Orange Park's 'Monkey Farm,'" *Florida Times-Union*, July 3, 2009.

Robert Yerkes, shown here with two chimpanzees, chose Orange Park as the site for his primate research, in part, because of the local climate. (Courtesy of Clay County Archives.)

But the lab opened in 1930. Yerkes ran the lab for its first decade. In 1965, it moved to Atlanta, where today it's called the Yerkes National Primate Research Center, funded by the National Institutes for Health.

Not much is publicly known about Donald Kellogg's later life, but in 1973, when he was 43 years old, he committed suicide.[114]

The Caretaker's House

Paradoxically, a Himalayan salt lamp glows a cool pink on the front counter. Nearby are shelves and shelves of locally produced honey, cartons of rice nog, assortments of vitamin pills, and bottles of yerba mate and ginger beer.

Nelson Hellmuth's mother had always loved the charming two-story house built in 1887. The expansion of the interstate system had brought massive suburban development to the little town of Orange Park, and older houses were frequently demolished. Orange Park Mall opened in 1975. Kingsley Avenue was widened, spawning rows of new commercial structures on either side of the street.

Nelson and Julie Hellmuth began The Granary, their whole foods retail shop, inside the old house in 1979. The house still has its original 130-year-old copper roof, the bluish green patina of which you can see from near the hickory tree that may be older than the house.

The house had been abandoned for two years. According to the few stories that survive, it spent 35 years as the Yerkes Laboratories' caretaker's house, and the rest of the '60s and early '70s as The Orange Door, a kind of halfway house whose inmates seem to have run the institution.

---

[114] Dewsbury, *Monkey Farm*, 100.

In his office at the back of the second floor, Nelson points to holes that remain in the doorjamb where four large latch bolts once locked an old door that weighed hundreds of pounds. He's sure this back office is where inmates' personal effects, and maybe confiscated drugs, were impounded. In The Granary's early years, former inhabitants of The Orange Door sometimes stopped by, usually surprised their former residence was gone.

Standing by the basement door, Nelson recalls the swarm of termites that rose from below when The Granary first opened. He points down the stairs to the brick and lath-and-plaster walls. The exterminator looked at the solid heart pine walls and beams of the old house and told him termites would have no interest in such hardwood with so much new construction nearby. In fact, the termites had been attracted to plywood stacked in the basement, and once the plywood was gone, the termites were too.

Nelson points to carved crosses on the upper corners of entryway doors and windows. They resemble the Confederate "Cross of Honor," which looks so much like the "Iron Cross" of the Nazis. On the backs of the same corners are carved circles.

An architect once told him the crosses facing the entrance were supposed to keep out evil, while the circles that greet you before you leave the house represented watchful and protective eyes.

Though the house preceded the Yerkes Lab by nearly half a century, my sister Wanda points out that its story arc from ape research to halfway house to health and whole foods store makes for a lovely and optimistic narrative.

Nelson also runs a solar power business, Solar Designs, from his back second-floor office: "Engineering and Design for all Things Solar." He shows us the upstairs kitchen and dining room where Julie taught cooking classes for 20 years.

The Hellmuths have seen generations of pregnant women shop The Granary for maternal care. Nelson says, "We'll get to know a pregnant woman who shops here, then she has her baby. They keep coming, and that baby grows up. Then she becomes the pregnant woman shopping here."

He smiles and says, "The best thing anyone has ever told me about this place. This woman had been shopping here for years, and she said, 'Every time I'm in this house, something just comes over me, and I'm happy here.'"

Models for "Mental Engineering"

Orange Park today is less its own entity apart from Jacksonville than it was when the Monkey Farm opened in 1930. Though the town still retains distinctive elements that identified it before the post-World War II suburban boom, much of Orange Park and its environs blend seamlessly with the billboard-littered asphalt and rows of fast food establishments that sprawl across outer Jacksonville.

Just as many Jacksonville residents never experience their own city's most distinctive and historic urban streets and neighborhoods, Northeast Floridians often miss Orange Park's oak-shaded midcentury-modern houses, its lovely riverside groves, and the 19th-century houses pocketed in late 20th-century suburban developments.

When Yale chose Orange Park as the ideal location for Robert Yerkes's lab, the town more closely resembled the rustic community that had named itself for the citrus industry in 1877.[115]

A thousand miles south of Yale, this Southern town with a 1930 population of 661 might seem an unlikely location for an

---

[115] Dewsbury, *Monkey Farm*, 63.

Ivy League research outpost, but historical paths wend strangely, impossible to predict.

In 1916, *Science* published a paper Yerkes wrote in which he called for a research center dedicated to studying primates' "fundamental instincts" and "social relations."[116]

Florida's climate—hot and humid, if not quite equatorial Africa—seemed best suited to harboring gorillas, bonobos, and spider chimpanzees.

Yerkes and Yale considered Sarasota, Jacksonville, and Gainesville outside the University of Florida, but chose Orange Park partly because it offered the cheapest land close to significant railroad lines in a most remote location, offering "security for the animals," but also anonymity for research.[117]

As Mary Jo McTammany put it humorously in her "Clay County Memoirs" newspaper column,

> The new arrivals were northeastern urban academics, highly educated and accustomed to taking things like paved streets, fenced livestock and indoor plumbing for granted.[118]

Of Orange Park's 250 homes, not quite a third had electricity. In 1939, Ada Yerkes, Robert's wife, wrote a monograph called "Yale in Florida," in which she complained of "pigs and cattle" as a "menace to the unwary motorist."[119]

Scientist Karl Lashley complained that in the 1950s, he had to travel to Jacksonville for "intellectual contacts," which, even in the larger city, were "few." He recalled San Marco's

---

[116] Robert M. Yerkes, "Provision for the Study of Monkeys and Apes," *Science* 43 (1916): 231-234.
[117] Dewsbury, *Monkey Farm*, 63.
[118] Mary Jo McTammany, "Mysterious 'Farm' Lives on in Name," *Florida Times-Union*, March 4, 1998.
[119] Dewsbury, *Monkey Farm*, 66.

"Little Theatre, a second-rate symphony, a starting university [Jacksonville University] graduating its first class next year." Scientist Marilyn Ferster Gilbert, who thought of the South itself as "a wasteland," remembered seeing "the separate water fountains when we went to Jacksonville, but little else."[120]

With his interest in eugenics and fear of "race deterioration," Yerkes would have been untroubled by the racial oppression everywhere evident in the Jim Crow South.

As the creator of intelligence tests for the U.S. Army during World War I, Yerkes had sought to define intelligence in terms of culture and race. Because the Army's tests largely measured acculturation, recent American immigrants scored as less "intelligent." Yerkes and other eugenicists consistently misperceived cultural understanding relative to genetics. A post-war report by Yerkes and his associates concluded, "If we may safely judge by the Army measurements of intelligence, races are quite as significantly different as individuals."

Yerkes's obituary claims he was "especially interested in psychobiological research, mental engineering and problems of population."[121]

In his 1943 book, *Chimpanzees: A Laboratory Colony*, Yerkes proposed the mental engineering of primates as a model for imagining what might be done with humans.

"[T]he effort to create an ideally suitable laboratory chimpanzee," Yerkes writes, "may prove useful to those who are seeking an ideal for mankind." Offering an extensive list of "human shortcomings," including "extreme selfishness" and "slothfulness," Yerkes argues that "developing an ape" with

---

[120] Ibid., 221.
[121] "Robert Yerkes Dies, Noted in Biology Field," *New York Times*, Feb. 5, 1956.

higher levels of "dependability" and "cooperativeness" could serve to "shame a portion of our kind" toward realizing the "modifiability, controllability, and consequent improvability, of human nature."[122]

It's hard not to conclude that besides climate, nearby railroads and other reasons for situating the lab in Orange Park, this small rural Deep South town's social and cultural climate might have served equally well.

Questions for Bokar

Just east of The Granary is an office complex where newer stucco-fronted buildings stand beside older concrete structures.

At first glance, the buildings seem nearly identical, but strange holdovers from previous existences linger amidst today's Christian marital counseling offices. On three separate buildings, original to the Monkey Farm, old outside iron stairs lead into windows on the second floor, impossible to open. One set of stairs leads from a window to a drop in midair.

Along the walkways between buildings stand iron posts painted innocuous beige and yellow. Around the periphery, old fences still wear crowns of barbed wire, and electrical sockets and conductors from 65 years ago hide in the vines that have overgrown the pines.

These concrete-walled buildings that so blend in with the newer 1970s and '80s stucco facades once housed chimpanzees, gibbons, and gorillas. Side walkways once held open-air cages. The tops of walkways lead to iron stairs that lead to unopenable windows, because the windows once were doors, and the roofs of

[122] Robert M. Yerkes, *Chimpanzees: A Laboratory Colony* (Oxford: Oxford University Press, 1943), 9-11.

walkways once were second-floor walks that circumnavigated the laboratory complex.

The stairs between windows and midair remind me of *l'esprit d'escalier*, the ghost of stairways, the haunting of the thing you should have said or done at a certain turning of your life, which you realized only too late. In a 1930 poem "Ash Wednesday," T.S. Eliot calls the spirit "the devil of the stairs who wears / the deceitful face of hope and of despair."

Building names all relate to the Yerkes Labs' funding. The Yale Building, the Stetson Building, and the Carnegie Building are original to the Monkey Farm. Marvin Wilhite, the developer who built the nearby Foxwood subdivision and this office complex, headquartered here, calling his company Ahpla, Inc., spelling backward the name of the first chimp born at Yerkes. Alpha was born on September 11, 1930.

I'm looking for Bokar, the lovely chimpanzee who held to the top of his cage and opened his mouth for the primatologist to check his teeth in 1951. Don't call a chimpanzee a monkey. He might take great offense.

I want to ask Bokar what he thought, 66 years ago, of the spider monkeys and macaques nearby. I'd ask him at midday, so he'd already have had his breakfast of apples, carrots, sweet potatoes, grapes, orange slices, and bread.

The infants in the nursery upstairs have been bottle-fed their morning milk.

I have for Bokar bananas, which he usually eats in the morning, and a head of cabbage, which he usually takes for lunch.[123] I'm going to find him. I'm going to ask him what he thought.

---

[123] Dewsbury, *Monkey Farm*, 180.

I'm going to ask him about halfway houses and Himalayan salt lamps. Then I'm going to see what I think when instead of his speaking my English, my communication patterns change to chimp vocalizations.

Selected References

Dewsbury, Donald *A. Monkey Farm: A History of the Yerkes Laboratories of Orange Park, Florida, 1930-1965*. Lewisburg: Bucknell University Press, 2005.

Kellogg, W.N. "Humanizing the Ape," *Psychological Review*, 38, 2, March 1931.

——— and L.A. Kellogg, *The Ape and the Child: A Study of Environmental Influence Upon Early Behavior*. New York: McGraw-Hill, 1933.

Yerkes, Robert M. *Chimpanzees: A Laboratory Colony*. Oxford: Oxford University Press, 1943.

Grady Smith purchased an ice plant in Green Cove Springs in 1928. Two years later, he bought the town's Coca-Cola bottling plant from owner E.E. Geiger. (Courtesy of Clay County Archives.)

Ice and a Coca-Cola

Marshall Lenne

The first time I saw the Green Cove Springs Senior Center in 2012, I immediately considered my age. The building was worn, like me; its paint matched my hair, white with dappled spots of gray. The building had seen better days as a Coca-Cola bottling plant. A few months later my wife and I visited our old home in Tennessee. A friend asked, "Is the old Coca-Cola plant still there?" My answer—yes and no. The building remained, but not the Coca-Cola. This answer ricocheted in my mind when I returned to Clay County, and new questions emerged. What was the history of the building? What does its future hold?

Back in September 1911, a cold-storage journal carried a one-line entry, "Green Cove Springs will erect an ice plant."[124] It was built on the north side of Center Street next to the railroad tracks. Four years later, *Refrigerating World* reported:

> Green Cove Springs—Citizens of this city are discussing the advisability of purchasing the ice plant here, now owned and operated by private parties. The idea is to consolidate the ice plant with that of the light and water plant, and make it a municipally owned and operated proposition.[125]

---

[124] *Cold Storage and Ice Trade Journal*, 42-43 (Sept. 1911): 48.
[125] *Refrigerating World Incorporating Cold Storage & Ice Trade Journal*, 32, 2 (1915): 42.

I found no documentation that this ever occurred.

The ice wagon, a familiar sight, back on city streets and Clay County roads, delivered block ice to city and county residents. Ice wagons became an American institution. They delivered ice to consumers who posted an 'Ice Today' sign in their windows. Iceboxes, typically made of wood, lined with tin or zinc, and insulated with sawdust or seaweed, preserved meat and vegetables. The ice melted into pans underneath, which had to be emptied daily.[126]

According to his daughter, Mildred Kinnear, E.E. Geiger founded the Cove Springs Bottling Works in 1913, first housed in a small sheet metal building on West Center Street's north side.

> First deliveries of bottled drinks, which included cream soda, orange, strawberry, and sarsaparilla, as well as Coca-Cola, were made by large horse-drawn wagons. Bottled drinks were delivered to merchants in Green Cove ... [deliveries] to outlying areas, Doctor's Inlet, Orange Park and West Tocoi [went] by way of railroad freight.[127]

Cases of 24 bottles were used for local deliveries, while the railroad carried "large coffin-like containers" of 144 bottles.[128]

The bottles were recycled. Returned bottles entered a soaker, bathed in "a hot caustic soda solution" emerging "sparkling clean." The Geiger boys, Park, Wayne, and Bill,

---

[126] "Ice Box," Wikipedia, https://en.wikipedia.org/wiki/Icebox.
[127] Mildred Kinnear, personal notes, no date, from a copy provided to Frank Haggard, Atlantic Reserve Fleet historian.
[128] Ibid.

handled this process "as soon as they were big enough to reach it with the help of an empty bottle crate."[129]

Mrs. Kinnear's notes reveal the old plant had two floors:

> The syrups for the sodas were made and mixed with concentrated flavors on the upper floor of [the] building and fed to hand-operated bottling machines via copper tubing and gravity. The bottling machine was on the first floor. Sometimes, in mixing the syrup and carbonated water, a flavored bottle would reach the bottling machine, with the result [of] broken glass flying everywhere. All three boys had scars testifying to this, Bill having the most.[130]

The initial recipe for Coca-Cola included coca leaf derivatives, but that recipe changed before 1930. After this, the mixed syrup arrived in wooden barrels marked in big red letters "Cocaine Removed."[131]

> About the time of moving the plant across to the south side of Center Street, the old horse-drawn wagon(s) were put 'out to pasture,' and Mr. Geiger bought a Model T Ford truck for deliveries … one of the first trucks in Green Cove had a capacity of 60 cases of 24 bottles each. The bottling company was among the first in Florida to bottle Coca-Cola.[132]

---

[129] Ibid.
[130] Ibid.
[131] Interview, Jean Dickason, administrative assistant, Clay Council on Aging, Feb. 2015.
[132] Kinnear, personal notes.

Coke delivery truck, shown here stacked with wooden cases, parked across the street from the bottling plant. (Courtesy of Clay County Archives.)

Grady Smith, his wife Edna, and their two children, Jim and Marguerite, came to Green Cove Springs in November 1928 from Benton, Arkansas, where Grady worked for various utility companies.[133] In 1929 Grady purchased the ice plant and went into business.[134] Later that year, the world changed. On October 29, a day we still call Black Tuesday, the stock market collapsed; billions of dollars, the savings and investments of thousands of people, were lost. Jobs dried up. In 1930, unemployment nearly tripled from the year before, to 8.9 percent. By 1933, it reached 25 percent—one in four workers could not find jobs.[135]

Florida fared little better. A Mediterranean fruit fly invasion in 1929 decimated the citrus crop; production dropped 60 percent. By the early 1930s, 26 percent of Floridians depended on public relief to survive, yet migrant workers continued to come, often because they'd lost their homes elsewhere.[136]

During the winter months, tourism bolstered Florida's flagging economy a bit. Visitors from nearby states came to enjoy the climate. Some came hoping to leave the cold and destitution behind. Due to hard economic times, Florida stationed state police at its border to make sure people seeking entrance had enough money or a job to support them. If not, they were turned away.[137]

---

[133] Ann Williamson, *Clay County Leader*. Sept. 28-Oct. 4, 1994.

[134] Mary Jo McTammany, "Coca-Cola a Big Part of Everyday Life in Clay County." *Clay Today*, Oct. 4, 2012.

[135] Lawrence W. Reed, "Great Myths of the Great Depression" Mackinac Center for Public Policy, Atlanta Georgia, https://mackinac.org/archives/1998/sp1998-01.pdf.

[136] Florida Center for Instructional Technology, "Great Depression and the New Deal, Exploring Florida: A Social Studies Resource for Students and Teachers," University of South Florida, 2002. https://fcit.usf.edu/florida/lessons/depress/depress1.htm.

[137] Ibid.

In the face of this economic environment, how did Grady Smith respond? "On his birthday in 1930, Grady bought the Coca-Cola plant from E.E. Geiger."[138]

He moved the bottling plant to property next to the ice plant to create a side-by-side operation. Some employees worked in both plants. They usually started their day about 2:00 a.m. "pulling" ice blocks, then worked in the bottling plant until about nine in the morning. After that, drivers delivered ice to homes and businesses. Grady drove a truck and sold Coca-Cola products to area merchants and vendors. "Neither business could have made it through the depression separately."[139]

Refrigerators were not yet a household item. Instead, most families owned an ice box that required regular ice deliveries. To reduce operating expenses, "Grady, like other bottlers, paid for the return of empty bottles. The first cash ever earned by many a youngster growing up in Clay County came from collecting bottles for the deposit."[140]

In 1936, at age 16, Grady's son Jim joined the family business as a salesman with a truck route.[141] Grady now had two ice drivers and two soft drink drivers, along with a few laborers who worked only in the plants. Coca-Cola runs expanded to include St. Augustine, Jacksonville Beach, and Daytona Beach.[142]

> When Jim loaded his truck, he would first load the bottles, and then he would cover them with 15 to 20 canvas bags of ice from the ice plant. When

[138] Williamson, Clay County Leader.
[139] Dickason interview.
[140] McTammany, "When Coca-Cola."
[141] Williamson, Clay County Leader.
[142] Dickason interview.

> he delivered the soft drinks, he would sell the retailers ice to keep the beverages cold.[143]

According to Calvin Wilcox,

> The plants were located near the Center Street railroad crossing. The train depot was on Ferris Street and only a few blocks from Center Street. The trains slowed or stopped at the depot. Kids hopped on the trains, rode the few blocks to Center Street crossing, and jumped off at the plants to get ice chips or a Coca-Cola. The ice prices varied from seven cents for small blocks to 25 cents for larger blocks.[144]

Life had its sweet moments, despite the Depression. Then the unthinkable happened.

December 7, 1941, just before 8:00 a.m., hundreds of Japanese fighter-bombers attacked the American naval base at Pearl Harbor near Honolulu, Hawaii. The devastating barrage lasted two hours. The Japanese destroyed nearly 20 American naval vessels, including eight enormous battleships and almost 200 planes. Over 2,000 Americans soldiers and sailors died and another 1,000 were wounded. The next day, President Franklin D. Roosevelt asked Congress to declare war on Japan. Congress approved his declaration with just one dissenting vote. Three days later, Japanese allies Germany and Italy declared war on the

---

[143] Ibid.

[144] Interview, Calvin Wilcox, Green Cove Springs resident.

U.S., and again Congress reciprocated. More than two years into the conflict, the U.S. joined World War II (WWII).[145]

> During the first world war, Jacksonville Naval Air Station used Benjamin Lee Field in Green Cove Springs as a Naval Pilot Training Auxiliary Base. In World War II, the base became a full-fledged Naval Air Station to train pilots for the war effort. The war effort brought an influx of new people to Clay County, in particular, to Green Cove Springs. Grady secured the vending rights to supply Coca-Cola drinks to Benjamin Lee Field. He assigned his son, Jim, responsibility for the new Naval Air Station.[146]

During WWII, Jim made runs to Lee Field every night, returning in the early morning hours to catch a few hours of sleep before starting over in the plant. Eventually, coin-operated commercial refrigeration units were available for lease from Coca-Cola bottlers, and Jim began refilling and maintaining these units throughout the Naval Air Station.[147]

The end of WWII brought more changes. The United States Navy decided to store or "mothball" a vast number of warships at Green Cove Springs. In preparation for this new mission, Lee Field, a wartime auxiliary airfield for Jacksonville Naval Air Station, underwent major alterations.

> In 1946, thirteen 1,500-foot concrete piers were built into the St. Johns River, at the cost of $10

[145] "Pearl Harbor," http://history.com/topics/world-war-ii/pearl-harbor.
[146] Williamson, Clay County Leader.
[147] Dickason interview.

> million, to securely house the U.S. Naval Atlantic Reserve or "Mothball Fleet" of WWII. At its height, over 600 vessels, primarily destroyers, destroyer escorts, and fleet auxiliaries, were stationed at Green Cove Springs, along with more than 5,000 naval personnel and 1,000 civilian employees.[148]

The Atlantic Reserve Fleet historian clarified this history:

> Seven hundred thirty-three ships were anchored in the St. Johns River from Doctor's [Lake] down to Green Cove Springs. Some would be scrapped, and others would be mothballed in case they were needed again.[149]

The influx of construction and permanent Navy personnel to undertake this project presented greater opportunities for Grady Smith. He knew he needed to expand and modernize his operations. He secured the funds to build a state-of-the-art bottling plant, which he relocated to the corner of Pine and Walnut Streets in Green Cove Springs. In 1946, the *Florida Times-Union* reported the construction cost at $75,000.00. The article described the new facility as one of the finest examples of a modern Coca-Cola bottling plant in the Southeast. Its first floor contained the main bottling room, administrative offices, maintenance shop, and garage. The second floor held the syrup room.[150]

---

[148] "Exploring Clay County Port/Reynolds Park," http://metrojacksonville.com/.../2010-nov-exploring-clay-county-port-reynolds-park.

[149] Interview, Frank Hayward.

[150] "Green Cove Springs Gets New Plant." *Florida Times-Union*, April 7, 1946.

The modern architecture with large glass windows offered passersby a view of the bottling process. Calvin Wilcox recalls how spellbound youngsters and oldsters, too, watched mesmerized as bottles traveled through the process, filled with syrup, topped off with carbonated water, capped, then loaded into cases for delivery.[151]

George Wyman's father owned a grocery store in Green Cove Springs and bought his Coca-Cola from Grady. George said,

> In the old days, Mark Green delivered ice to the store. Eventually, my father used commercial refrigeration to cool soft drinks. Grady paid for return of the glass Coke bottles. He washed, inspected, sanitized and refilled the returned bottles.[152]

[151] Interview, Calvin Wilcox
[152] Interview, George Wyman, Feb. 2015.

Grady Smith inside his bottling plant. Mary Jo McTammany wrote, “In 1971, after four decades of supplying Clay County with ‘a Coke and a smile,’ Smith closed the business down.” (Courtesy of Clay County Archives.) http://jacksonville.com/tu-online/stories/102004/nec_16939444.shtml#.Wc6lENFryUk

Another longtime Clay resident, Marlene Foy, fondly recalls returning Coca-Cola bottles to Wyman's store for money to buy popsicles in the heat of summer.[154]

Grady, his son, Jim, and daughter Marguerite operated the Coca-Cola Bottling Plant until 1971, when Coke began reducing the number of bottling franchises nationwide.[155] Also, new packaging technology required new equipment. After more than four decades of supplying businesses and residents with bottled Coca-Cola products, Grady Smith closed the Green Cove Springs plant.[156]

According to Betty Battle, for a time the space served as a warehouse for Coca-Cola products. Then Sam's Garage operated out of the building, before the operation moved closer to the center of Green Cove Springs.[157]

Clay County purchased the building in 1980 and turned it into a senior center. Over the years grants and private donations funded a major renovation and addition to the structure. The original building at the corner of Pine and Walnut was integrated into the headquarters of Council on Aging Clay (COAC), a full-service center for senior citizens. Clay Transit, kitchen facilities, and adult day care now occupy space in the former bottling plant.

---

[154] Interview, Marlene Foy, Feb. 2015.
[155] Mary Jo McTammany "Coca-Cola a Big Part."
[156] Ibid.
[157] Interview, Betty Battle.

The one-time Coca-Cola bottling plant now serves as a senior center at 604 Walnut Street. (Courtesy of Clay County Archives.)

The COAC has three other locations—Orange Park, Middleburg, and Keystone Heights—providing services to ensure Clay seniors live with dignity and independence. For example, in 2015, the COAC:

Transported 135,500 riders.

Delivered nearly 22,000 meals to homes.

Hosted over 47,500 visits at four centers.

Distributed over 8,000 bags of commodities.

Provided 33,471 hours of licensed daycare.

Completed 37,980 hours of in-home services.

The many ongoing events and activities at local COAC centers enhance the well-being and enrich the lives of seniors and adults with disabilities in Clay.[158]

What started as two small businesses that provided employment and consumer products for local people from 1911-1913, grew through the years, moving from one building to another. Now the last building has morphed again into a facility that brings renewed life to so many people.

Why not visit and see for yourself what happens at the COAC center in Green Cove Springs, Florida?

---

[158] Annual Board of Directors presentation report, Council on Aging Clay, May 2016.

Exterior of Penney Memorial Church. As a minister's son, J.C. Penney recognized the hardships clergy and missionaries often faced when they retired. He commissioned this Norman-style place of worship in honor of his parents. It was the first structure completed in the Memorial Home Community. (Photo by Jay Moore.)

Dreams and Legacies: Penney Farms and the Penney Retirement Community

Nancy Moore

This story begins with the name of one man, but it is the story of many. That man, J.C. Penney, opened his first shop in Kemmerer, Wyoming in 1902. By the 1920s, he was a department-store magnate operating stores across the country; his name, a household word. In 1926, with a new vision in mind, he took advantage of the end of Florida's land boom to buy property and establish a unique community. He invited people to live and work in Clay County. Eager to find rosier prospects, many responded to his offer.

Early Days and Significant Events

Before Penney Farms, the Florida Farms and Industries Company (FIAC) had settled an unincorporated area known as Long Branch City, west of Green Cove Springs. By 1918, Long Branch had a few farms, a school, the St. Johns Hotel, a canning factory, company store, and post office—as well as a rail system. In October 1921, the Bordenville Dairy Farm and Camphor Farm also provided employment.

But things did not go as planned. By 1923, many farmers and workers moved away, discouraged by Clay's sandy soil and hot weather.[159] Finally, the FIAC was forced to sell. As a prospective buyer, J.C. Penney anticipated a prosperous investment and an opportunity to establish a model farming operation. But a deeper motivation began years before, derived from the parents who shaped his life with their Christian faith and practice.

James Cash Penney, Sr. and his wife, Mary Frances raised a family of 12 children in Hamilton, Missouri, where they farmed 390 acres with cattle and crops. Their seventh child, James Cash, was born in 1875. Money was tight, but in addition to farming, the elder Penney faithfully volunteered as pastor of a Primitive Baptist Church.[160] After 20 years, when he finally asked for financial support and added his conviction that pastors should receive further education, he was dismissed from church membership. This bitter experience influenced Penney's eventual desire to create a memorial to his parents' lives—a haven where Christian ministers in active retirement could find financial security and continue to use their skills.

Focused solely on his businesses, Penney initially worked seven days a week to establish department stores all over the country. But the deaths of his first wife, Berta, and the second, Mary, left him grieving to raise his three sons alone. During a cruise to Europe and the Holy Land, his spiritual advisor, the Rev. Dr. Francis Short, encouraged him to reflect on his faith in God and to adopt a broader, more philanthropic approach to life.[161]

---

[159] Arch Fredric Blakey, *Parade of Memories, A History of Clay County, Florida*, (Clay County, Fla.: Board of County Commissioners, 1976), 210.
[160] Orlando Tibbetts, *The Spiritual Journey of J.C. Penney* (Danbury, Conn.: Rutledge Books, Inc., 1999), 5.
[161] Phillip A. Werndli, "J.C. Penney and the Development of Penney Farms," Master's thesis, University of Florida, Gainesville, 1974, 21.

Known for a keen interest in honest and successful business practices, Penney frequently spoke with farmers who came to his stores. Isolated in rural areas, many lacked the knowledge for effective farming. When doctors advised him to "get more fresh air," he began planting crops and raising dairy cattle on his estate in White Plains, New York.[162]

Two Dreams: Seizing the Opportunity

Meanwhile in Clay, the Florida Farms and Industries Company failed, and in 1924, its land was sold at public auction. Penney saw the advantages: nearby railroad system, busy waterways, local forestry, the dairy industry, and the popularity of Green Cove Springs as a healthful tourist destination. Here was a place he could build the two dreams he brought with him: to establish first, an independent, model-farming cooperative, and second, a fully-endowed retirement community for pastors, missionaries, and YMCA workers.[163]

Penney's partner in the 1924 venture was J.C. Penney Company attorney Ralph Gwinn. Together they purchased 120,000 acres of Clay County farmland between Green Cove Springs and Starke for $400,000. Two Green Cove Springs hotels—the St. Elmo and the Qui Si Sana ("Here Is Health")—were included with the purchase.

A Change in Plans

To house the farming families, he had planned to renovate 35 run-down lumbermen's cottages near the mill on the St. Johns River. After further consideration, Penney decided these

---

[162] Ibid., 22, 27.

[163] Tibbetts, *The Spiritual Journey,* 53.

families deserved something better—homes built for them in Long Branch City. Penney intended to erect a large building—100 three-room apartment units in Green Cove Springs—to house Christian ministers. The community objected to the potential for traffic congestion and "too many old people."

Instead, in 1926, Penney set aside 60 acres for the Memorial Home Community, which included 22 furnished retirement cottages. The chartered legal purpose of this community was inherent in its very provision and in its contribution to "usefulness in longer living." In 1927, the Chapel dedicated to his parents was the first building to be erected, registering 100 members from 19 separate Protestant denominations.[164] That year, Penney married his third wife, Caroline, with whom he would have two daughters.

By 1927, the Town of Penney Farms included 20,000 cleared acres, 300 buildings, a general store, post office, garage and machine shop, a canning factory, a boarding house, a dairy farm, and 3,000 range cattle. By 1928, 58 families responded to Penney's advertisements for farmers who were serious, stable and mature. The town had a railroad spur line to haul barrels of turpentine, cans of milk, farm produce, beef, pork, chickens, and the U.S. mail. Such items were destined for markets in Green Cove, St. Augustine, Jacksonville, and other cities via the Florida East Coast Railway. To encourage scientific farming, Penney built an Agricultural Institute. There, students pored over studies of soil testing and drainage, the suitability of seed and fertilizer, the latest methods for raising crops, and the improvement of livestock.[165]

---

[164] Ibid., 97-98.
[165] Werndli, "J.C. Penney," 54-57.

Two views of the Colonial Inn, once a gateway to Penney Farms. (Upper) Colonial Inn amid the early layout of streets in Penney Farms. (Lower) A 1930s W.P.A. project, it was constructed from used bricks and other second-hand building materials. Once considered a fine example of Colonial Revival architecture, the last public event celebrated there is thought to be the 1976 U.S. bicentennial. (Both views courtesy of Clay County Archives.) http://archives.clayclerk.com/the-hotel-era/

The Wheel Turns

For three years, farmers and their families seemed to do well, but certain challenges became unmanageable. The soil was too sandy, requiring large quantities of costly fertilizer. Distribution to markets near and far was inefficient, so produce often spoiled. Farmers fought the effects of pests and heat upon their crops. Construction of the Memorial Home Chapel and other buildings siphoned off men who were tired of the intensity of farm labor and wanted steadier wages. Finally, the realities of the Depression settled in. Facing bankruptcy, Penney could no longer financially undergird either the farming project or the retired Christian workers in his Memorial Home Community. By 1930, many of the farming families and 32 of the 90 retired ministers had been forced to leave.[166]

Paul Reinhold, owner of Foremost Dairies, had joined Penney's original venture. Saving Penney from further financial ruin, Reinhold stepped in and bought the remainder of the 120,000 acres originally intended for farming, timber, and cattle. Through his company, now called the Reinhold Corporation, he managed Shadowlawn Tree Farms and Nurseries, raised cattle, and became prominent in the dairy industry.

Help arrived for the retirees, as well. Because Penney had been a benefactor to Dr. Daniel Poling, editor of *The Christian Herald* publication, and to its Foundation, Poling agreed to oversee the continuation of the Memorial Home Community.[167]

Ruin or Recovery?

Penney's fortunes sank during the early 1930s, a devastating outcome for one who gave generously of his personal

---

[166] Ibid., 99, 105.
[167] Tibbetts, *The Spiritual Journey,* 71-72.

fortune to help so many people. Unable to pay his bills, he was forced to close his estates and ask for a salary from his company. He couldn't eat or sleep. He suffered from the shingles virus, finally endured a complete physical collapse, and was placed in a sanitarium. Sedated for days to rest his mind and body, he awoke one morning, hungry for breakfast. Wandering downstairs and hearing music, he found a small group worshiping in the chapel. Joining them, he experienced a renewed and very personal faith. By 1935, his fortunes were gradually being restored.[168]

How did the town and the Memorial Home Community survive the Depression without Penney's help? Retirees began paying a monthly fee for their cottages. Residents found work plowing or clearing land, grading roads, doing carpentry or maintenance, laundering clothes or dressmaking; and raising food in community gardens or on their farms. Fishing and hunting deer, rabbits, and wild pigs provided resources for the table and some residents kept cows and chickens. Others residents couldn't manage, and the population fell from its high, 825 in 1930, to a low of 370 by 1940.[169]

In the early 1940s, as the United States prepared to enter World War II, Camp Blanding expanded. Military personnel and their families poured into Jacksonville, Orange Park, Penney Farms, and Green Cove Springs. Cottages on Lewis Avenue became officers' quarters. The Colonial Inn at the corner of County Road 218 and State Road 16 was always full. The Works Progress Administration (WPA) built the stately hotel using materials salvaged from the old St. Johns Inn and the Agricultural Institute. That's where town residents held Sunday dinners, weddings, and receptions, and learned to be airplane spotters.

---

[168] Ibid., 140-142.
[169] Werndli, "J.C. Penney," 118, 137-139.

J.C. Penney had long been an advocate for scientific farming methods—much needed to grow crops in this area. The image here shows soil testing at Shadowlawn Farm in 1949. (Courtesy of the State Archives of Florida.)

With 10,000 buildings, Camp Blanding, known as Florida's fourth-largest city, provided work for many. Among other tasks, people from Penney Farms helped feed German, Japanese, and Italian prisoners of war there.[170]

Sprouting and Flourishing

The *Christian Herald Magazine* continued to publicize the Memorial Home Community, opened to Christian laypeople in the late 1940s. In 1950, the Herald Foundation finished the Quadrangle Apartments, which Penney had first envisioned for Green Cove Springs. The building included 120 apartments, a dining hall, lounge, infirmary and administration office. Gradually, retirement community operations were turned over to residents, and in the early 1970s, the name was changed to Penney Retirement Community (PRC). Eight superintendents contributed leadership and made improvements to the community from 1933 to 2000.[171] Robert Rigel, the first professional CEO, served 2001 to 2014, succeeded by Teresa Scott, the present CEO.

Improvements to PRC included single family homes, an arts and crafts center, Barrows Assembly Hall, and a Commons with fitness center, swimming pool, coffee shop, and library. In addition, PRC has a nursing home (The Pavilion), a memory-care unit (Hagen), wellness and rehabilitation clinic, two assisted-living buildings, and Mobility Worldwide, a non-profit factory that produces vehicles for the disabled.

As PRC's infrastructure improved, so did that of Penney Farms: the Town Hall enlarged, roads upgraded, damaged trees

---

[170] Katherine "Elaine" Fullerton Williamson, *Community Memories*, commemorative publication, Penney Farms, Fla., 2002, 5-17.
[171] Tibbetts, *The Spiritual Journey*, 132-133.

removed, new trees planted, and a new wastewater system installed. The Historical Society was established in 2004. In 2006, after a substantial gift from an anonymous corporate donor and labor donated by New York State sculptor, Dexter Benedict, a statue of J.C. Penney was erected in front of Town Hall.[172]

This quiet town brings together enterprising people from all walks of life, who have worked in farming, landscaping, construction services, teaching, the health professions, social services, legal services, business and office management, law enforcement, auto services, hairstyling, the military, and pastoral care.[173] Town residents and retirees take turns in municipal duties. In 2017, Adrian Andrews succeeded Thomas DeVille as mayor.

The Legacy

A board of directors and 169 employees support PRC. Along with their work, staff contribute their personal care and dedication. Employees come from Penney Farms and other towns and counties in the area. Some have worked here 50 years or more. Some family members have joined them to work or live in the town or the retirement community.

Prompted by a core faith which values others through God's love, this community is widely recognized for its generosity and service. In 2016, retirees gave a total of 143,697 hours of service, benefiting their neighbors and the greater area. Such commitments include working at the mobility factory; supporting church benevolences; tutoring; guardian ad litem representation; foster care; assistance with income tax reporting;

---

[172] Beth Reese Cravey, "Bronze Statue of J.C. Penney Comes to His Town," *Florida Times-Union*. April 15, 2006.

[173] Interview with Tom DeVille, former Penney Farms mayor, Oct. 2016.

transportation services; safety patrol; monitoring the fitness center; producing online and printed community news; contributing to the Green Cove Food Bank; maintaining a busy resale outlet; serving on committees for the benefit of residents; membership on the Town Council; offering continuing education courses; contributing to resident aid; helping in the Pavilion and assisted-living buildings; and sponsoring the annual Crop Walk and 5K Run.[174]

Retirees participate in a residents' association, and may also sit on the Board of Directors. The community has embraced Christian workers of every kind of background, from aviation and business to teaching and publishing, engineering, design, and manufacturing, as well as education, missions, social work, pastoring, and preaching.[175]

At the heart of PRC, Penney Memorial Church incorporates 27 different denominational backgrounds, gives to many worldwide and local ministries, offers scholarships to deserving students, and sponsors free programs and concerts open to the public. The wealth of pastors and missionaries in retirement affords the congregation a different worship leader every week, four Sunday School classes, Tuesday Bible study, and Friday morning intercessory prayer, as well as healing prayer services and spiritual formation studies for small groups.

In 1970, the Arts, Crafts and Services Division was one of the earliest organizations housed in a dedicated building. Year-round, various groups are busy creating such items as stained glass, jewelry, ceramics and pottery, weavings, knitted items, paintings and drawings, photography, furniture and carvings,

---

[174] Martha Gale, *Penney For Your Thoughts* newsletter, Penney Farms, Fla., March 2017.

[175] Interview with Phyllis Turner, Penney Farms archivist, Nov. 2016.

pine-needle crafts, quilting, wreaths, sewn items, and decorative objects specific to Christmas. Every November, a Fall Sale is held. Residents also provide for the community such services as mending and alterations, picture-framing, upholstery, and the repair of furniture, small appliances, and electronics, computers, watches and clocks, golf carts, and bicycles.

Personal Energy Transportation, today called Mobility Worldwide, attracts volunteers from PRC and from the broader community. The not-for-profit outreach program benefits individuals who lost the use of their legs through disease, accident, or war. It was founded in 1994 by Larry and Laura Hills, former missionaries to Zaire (now Congo), Africa. The group produces sturdy, hand-propelled, three-wheeled carts shipped to 103 countries worldwide. In 2016, 286 volunteers donated 11,804 hours of service to this project and manufactured 824 mobility vehicles.[176]

A strong faith in God has blessed and sustained Penney Farms through the mutual efforts of the town, the retirement community, its administrators, and staff. Benefactors in these efforts include the Reinhold Foundation, the PRC board of directors, and the Christian Herald Foundation. PRC CEO Teresa Scott stated:

> What continues to be consistent is the love and caring that exists between our neighbors and all of us who serve the mission of this community where older adults in retirement live active and purposeful lives, having the value and security of a voice in all areas of operation.

[176] *Mobility Worldwide* newsletter. Penney Farms, Fla., Feb. 2017.

Statue of J.C. Penney who founded Penney Farms in the 1920s. Though not all his plans worked out, his legacy lives on in the spirit and community contributions of Penney Farms residents. (Photo by Jay Moore.)

God's Planter

Throughout his life, J.C. Penney maintained a close relationship with Penney Farms and visited as often as he could. He continued to serve on the PRC board of directors and expressed his faith by helping others. Though he received many honorary degrees and titles, such as retail genius, gentleman farmer, author, lecturer, world traveler. Perhaps most apt is "man with a thousand partners," the title of one of his autobiographies, written with Robert W. Bruere in 1931, alluding to his practice of encouraging employee profit-sharing and entrepreneurship.

Penney's business practices, his philanthropic vision, and his faith have benefited millions. His first foundation aided adoption agencies, homeless shelters, youth clubs, vocational schools, libraries, family guidance centers, missionary projects, peace organizations, and health clinics. After rebuilding his fortune, he established a second foundation and aided National 4-H Clubs, Junior Achievement, and the causes of community renewal, the environment, and world peace.[177] James Cash Penney died in New York City in February 1971.

In its 90th year, the town of Penney Farms and the Retirement Community continue to reflect these enduring mottoes: "Unity in Community" and "A Life More Abundant." With these mandates, we are all Penney's Partners. In its original plan, the farming venture may have failed, but the legacy of faith, generosity, and purpose remains.

---

[177] Rich Brott, "*Business People Who Gave Generously,*" http://richbrott.com.

Selected References

Blakey, Arch Fredric. *Parade of Memories, A History of Clay County, Florida*. Clay County, Fla.: Board of County Commissioners, 1976.

Hempstead, Alfred G. *The Golden Jubilee Celebration of Penney Retirement* Community. Julia A. Lacy, ed. Penney Farms, Fla.: Penney Retirement Community Association, 1975.

Hunt, Lois. *Our Lively Heritage*, DVD. Penney Farms, Fla., April 2016.

Walter, Morton, D., ed. *The Unique Farm Project of James C. Penney.* Green Cove Springs, Fla.: The J.C. Penney/Gwinn Corporation Farms, 1927.

Tibbetts, Orlando. *The Spiritual Journey of J.C. Penney.* Danbury, Conn.: Rutledge Books, Inc., 1999.

Werndli, Phillip A. "J.C. Penney and the Development of Penney Farms." Master's thesis, University of Florida, Gainesville, 1974.

Poster from *Zaat*, a science fiction movie filmed in 1970. Destined to become a cult film, *Zaat* was shot partly in Clay County. (Courtesy of Clay County Archives.)

How Hollywood Found its Way to Clay

Inez Holger

Google 'Clay County' and you'll find a few points of interest such as Black Creek and Doctor's Lake and a few details about population and size. Not much more. Wikipedia mentions Camp Blanding and the era of Green Cove Springs' old resort hotels. There is no mention of the mobsters and monsters, or of the prisoners and privates, of Clay's film industry. No mention of the time Clay posed as the country of Japan for a film, no mention of the visits by the famous director Ridley Scott. Yet the sinuous, tannin-stained Creek, the woodsy military Camp set at the edge of Kingsley Lake, the Mission-style resort hotel that served caviar, and scenic locations throughout the county have supplied the backdrop and extras for quite a few Hollywood films.

At first glance, Clay County pales in size and sites by comparison to its northern neighbor, Duval. The larger county comprised of Jacksonville and beach cities boasts a zoo, a ferry, the Dames Point Bridge, Jacksonville International Airport, Hanna Park, several universities, Epping Forest, Big Talbot Island, two active naval stations, Alexander Brest Planetarium, Kingsley Plantation, the Riverwalk, and 700 square miles of surf, sand, marsh, dunes, and roadways. Still, over the years, producers chose to film at a clay pit in Middleburg, at a barbershop in Green Cove Springs, and at other local sites. What drew filmmakers to Clay?

The lightly populated county spread out along U.S. 17 and Blanding is "like a diamond in the rough" according to film producer Janine Anzalone who produced and created the television series *Exposure*. The county has a 72,000-acre military training facility, a seaport, Victorian-style homes, docks on the St. Johns River, and 20 miles of Black Creek—a stand-in for any jungle scene required—and Anzalone found something Jacksonville didn't have. She found the small-town feel she needed for her television show in the quiet cities of Green Cove Springs and Orange Park. She also cited the high level of support and cooperation from residents and businesses, as well as production costs.[178]

"It's a great place to film," she said, "visually pretty. I'd love to see a film studio here. It would cost much less than Hollywood." Anzalone filmed at Green Cove's public park, at the police department, at a residence in Orange Park, and along area roads.

Considering the size of Clay County and its low level of visibility, how would a Hollywood film producer like Anzalone discover Clay's assets? The process of bringing filmmakers to any county in the state begins in Los Angeles.[179] A representative of Film in Florida sends new scripts to the Florida Office of Film and Entertainment in Tallahassee. That office forwards the material to the 68 film commissioners[180] throughout the state who then compete for possible sites based on what they read in the

---

[178] From an interview with Janine Anzalone, executive producer of *Exposure*.

[179] Process of procuring film production described in an interview with Carl Post, retired Clay County film commissioner.

[180] Number of commissioners provided by Jessica Sims, Florida Department of Economic Opportunity.

scripts. Several counties have more than one commissioner; other counties have none.

First Time Felon needed a Mississippi River flood scene in a small downtown location. Walnut Street in Green Cove Springs could work. *Tigerland* needed a Louisiana military training camp that prepared recruits for the swamps of Vietnam. Camp Blanding met the need. *Road Raiders* had to look like a Japanese naval base in 1942. The Clay County Port in Green Cove Springs, which once berthed over 600 ships for the military, would work well, or producers could use the abandoned Fleming Island Naval Outer Landing Field.

After reading the scripts and selecting potential sites, the county's film commissioner photographs the sites and builds a marketing package to send to the production company for consideration. The photos must be assembled quickly, according to former Clay County Commissioner Carl Post, because of competition from other counties and states submitting their site proposals.

Before Clay County's office existed, the Jacksonville Film Commission included sites from surrounding counties such as Clay in its proposals. Without anyone in Clay County to concentrate on drawing filmmakers to the area and to then direct producers to local goods and services when they did come, Duval County reaped most of the economic benefits.

The Clay County Film Office was established in 1989 and received a budget of $2,500 for its inaugural year to woo filmmakers to Clay. Carl Post served as commissioner from 1989 to 2001, competing with Duval's film office in Jacksonville for movie production dollars. Post hoped "to make the economic dollars stick" in his county. As a lifelong resident of Clay

County," he said, "I wanted funds due to Clay to come to the county instead of to Jacksonville."

Though 1989 saw the birth of Clay's own film commission, Clay began contributing to the entertainment industry in the era of silent films. In 1917, according to Hibernia resident and author Margaret Seton Fleming Biddle, black workers from Hibernia served as extras in an Alice Brady film. Seton, who wrote *Hibernia: The Unreturning Tide*, did not name the film, but the timing, according to Florida film historian Lisa Bradberry, suggests *Maternity*.[181] The silent film star Alice Brady came to St. Augustine to escape the winter weather in New York and finish scenes for the movie.

In 1920, Clay County native Richard Norman opened his silent film studio, Norman Studios, in Jacksonville. Born in Middleburg in 1891, Norman filmed several full-length movies with all-black casts when the film industry was as segregated as movie theaters. He respectfully avoided the clichéd stereotypes of the time.

As silent films gave way to the sound era, spotlights burned in the county in 1951 for the feature film *Under the Gun*.[182] A production lot in California and Qui-Si-Sana hotel in Green Cove Springs provided the settings for a mobster sentenced to a prison farm in Florida for killing a man. As Universal International Pictures filmed at the upscale hotel with its lush courtyard, loggia running along three sides, and palm trees lining the perimeter, the hometown Rideout Drive-in

---

[181] Bradberry consulted the archives of *Motography* magazine, Feb. 10, 1917.

[182] Two or more sources were used to verify each film listed in this article. Sources include location manager interviews, Internet Movie Database (IMDb) web site of films and their locations, and historical archives.

Theatre on County Road 220 lit the roadside with 16 mm films projected onto a sheet stretched between cars.[183]

A few years later, film producers found a less-expensive substitute for the Amazon River in the dense foliage of a narrow waterway in Clay. The *Creature from the Black Lagoon* allegedly took a dip in Black Creek for one scene in the 1954 movie filmed predominantly in Wakulla Springs and Silver Springs. According to Carl Post, the creature returned to the same area of the creek for *Revenge of the Creature*, filmed mainly in Jacksonville at the present location of the River City Brewing Company. The Black Creek haunt of the glassy-eyed creature was approximately one-half mile west of the Highway 17 bridge.

In 1971, Green Cove Springs welcomed the monster *Zaat* to town. The radioactive creature, described by movie reviewer Jake Tucker as "a cross between Bigfoot, a catfish, and a baboon," emerged from the St. Johns River and staggered down Green Cove's main street, breaking into Mayhugh Drugstore along the way.

"The people in Green Cove Springs were the most accommodating that I have ever worked with," said Ron Kivett, who helped write the script along with Don Barton of Barton Studios in Jacksonville. "They put electrical outlets on every pole on that street so we'd have enough light." According to Kivett, the fearsome monster's fur was an avocado green bathmat. The film has become a cult classic, released in Canada as well as across the U.S. It returned to northeast Florida at Jacksonville's Horror Fest in 2009 and 2011.

Movies made for television used settings in Clay in 1986 and 1987. *Vengeance: The Story of Tony Cimo* and *Illegally*

---

[183] "Films and Theaters," Clay County Archives, http://archives.clayclerk.com/films.html.

Yours filmed scenes at the old Courthouse in Green Cove Springs. Stacey Keach and Kathy Crosby starred in the 1986 television movie *Intimate Strangers* filmed on the dock at Club Continental in Orange Park.

The year 1989 not only ushered in the new film commission that wooed CBS to film *Road Raiders* on the abandoned WWII military airfield on Fleming Island, but also marked a venture by Brandon's Camera of Jacksonville to nurture filmmakers in northeast Florida. Ron Kivett, who helped develop the 1971 film *Zaat* in Green Cove, worked at Brandon's and inspired the project. Brandon's offered use of its studio and professional equipment to film 30-minute shorts to air on Channel 47's "Your Wildest Dreams, First Features from Young Film Makers."[184] The series lasted 13 episodes. One episode was filmed in Clay County. A monster came to town once again, nurturing future talent in its wake.

A small crew of young film producers from the region shot *The Hole in the Woods* on private property in Fleming Island.[185] The episode introduced a "seelith," a mythic monster which lived in a deep hole at the base of a tree by the St. John's River, down the road from the volunteer Fire Station 22 on Pine Avenue. One scene was shot at the general store by the Shands Bridge. According to Kivett, Sally Industries of Jacksonville made a monster arm to poke out of a hole in the ground. The monster killed two men, one of them named Carl Post, who volunteered at Station 22. Post, cast as 'Bubba,' became the film commissioner of Clay County.

---

[184] A copy of a reference letter for Carl Post from Brandon's Camera provided the series name.
[185] Carl Post provided a VHS copy of the film.

Another actor in the amateur film was Kent Lindsey, the local television celebrity known as Safari Sam from 1985 to 1998. Lindsey later performed in *GI Jane*, filmed at Camp Blanding. William Boston, who composed the musical score for *The Hole in the Woods* and several of the shorts, became a Hollywood composer for films such as *3:10 to Yuma, The Hurt Locker, Alien vs. Predator: Requiem*, and *Live Free or Die Hard.*[186]

After the mythic seelith left town, the pace of film production by major studios in Clay increased. From 1989 to 2013, the county's streets, historic buildings, waterways, and military facilities were included in over 20 movie productions, television series, and individual shows. (Film scouts strongly considered Clay for 1999 film, *The General's Daughter*, but Savannah won the bid.)[187] Producers use several locations, often across the country, to film a single project. In some instances, Clay was featured in just one small scene. The productions in the following list below with an asterisk were predominantly filmed in the county:[188]

In addition, Ford, Winn Dixie, Pic N' Save, Hair for Men, Eddie Farah, and Cadillac all used Clay as a location to shoot television commercials.[189]

A film shoot can bring a lot of money into a county—from thousands to millions of dollars. For example, *GI Jane*, filmed in 1995, created an economic impact for Clay County of

---

[186] IMDb, http://imdb.com/.
[187] Verified by Carl Post and location manager Tom Fallon.
[188] Projects made in Clay since 1989. Location managers Tom Fallon, Rick Ambrose, and Mitch Harbeson verified amount of filming produced in Clay. Harbeson reported two episodes of *America's Most Wanted* made in Clay, but I could not verify the dates.
[189] Per Vishitra Garig, archives specialist, Clay County Archives.

$15 million. The 13 episodes of *Safe Harbor*, which ran on WB in 1999, yielded over $1 million. The 2005 movie, *Things that Hang from Trees*, generated $300,000.[190]

Money spent around a film site adds up quickly. The major production *GI Jane* brought Camp Blanding $100,000 in revenues. People associated with the movie spent over $100,000 at a Lil' Champ store, $22,000 at the Inn at Ravines, $190,000 at Holiday Inn Orange Park, $40,000 at Nu-Life Painting, and $4,000 at Tom's RV Service of Middleburg. The one-hour photo lab at Eckerd's benefited, too, taking in $150. The physical therapist who treated cast member Jim Caviezel (who later starred in *The Passion of Christ* and *Person of Interest*) earned $1,500. Mr. Transmission in Orange Park fixed a Humvee for $1,800. Caterers, building supply companies, electricians, gas stations, and the local car wash—all earned money from lodging of cast and crew and from building the set.

Major productions *GI Jane*, *First Time Felon*, *Tigerland*, *Sunshine State*, *Basic*, and *Brenda Starr* also brought notable actors to quiet Clay County. Demi Moore, Viggo Mortensen, Omar Epps, Rob Lowe, Colin Farrell, Angela Bassett, Edie Falco, John Travolta, Samuel Jackson, and Brooke Shields came to "the diamond in the rough." So did Timothy Dalton who once played Bond. James Bond. Yes, that was Faith Hill at Cooter's Barbershop, Chaney's Restaurant, and 1st Presbyterian Church. And yes, said Mr. Post, that was Ridley Scott, the producer of *Alien*, *GI Jane*, *Black Hawk Down*, *Prometheus*, and *The Good Wife*, eating at Burger King years ago while discussing a possible second film in unassuming Clay.

---

[190] Economic figures from documents supplied by Carl Post, including permits and post-production surveys.

Movies & TV Shows Made in Clay[191]

1989 Road Raiders*
1994 Summertime Switch (ABC family movie)*
1995 G.I. Jane*
1995 Pointman (television series)
1996 Sudden Terror: The Hijacking of School Bus #1
1996 Cold Case "Deer Hunter Murders" (a CBS episode)
1997 First Time Felon
1999 Bulldozer Baby (BBC documentary)
1999 Safe Harbor (WB television series)*
2000 Tigerland*
2001 Boot Camp (FOX reality show)*
2002 Sunshine State
2003 Basic
2004 Brenda Starr
2004 Manchurian Candidate
2005 Things that Hang From Trees
2011 Extreme Home Makeover (with Ty Pennington)
2011 Lifetime unnamed TV pilot
2012 Comics Open
2012 Exposure (television series)
2014 Ghostbuster (one episode on SyFy)
2014 Hopscotch
2014 Christmas Wedding Baby (independent film)

Artists Who Made Music Videos in Clay

1995 Ugly Kid
1999 Faith Hill
2010 Warriors of Poseidon
2013 Roscoe Bandana

[191] "Films and Theaters," http://archives.clayclerk.com/films.html.

The clay pit in Middleburg that Demi Moore crawled through for *G.I. Jane* is covered with homes now—Ravines Crossing. So is the Fleming Island airstrip that stood in for a Japanese military base in *Road Raiders*. But the state forests, the lakes, the creeks, the Victorian homes, the small towns of Green Cove Springs, Orange Park, and Middleburg, the old seaport, and the sprawling military camp known as Blanding that fans out from the perfectly round Kingsley Lake in southwest Clay, await the next film. Production-friendly Clay has it all.

Selected References

Andino, Alliniece T. "Comeback Role in Works for an Old Movie Legend: It May Not Be 'The End' for Norman Film Studios." *Florida Times-Union*, May 20, 2002.

"Film Liaisons," http://filmflorida.com/liaisonsmaps.cfm.

FitzRoy, Maggie. "Norman Studios." *First Coast Magazine*, Mar. 2015.

Wilson, Cristin. "Houses Can Be Movie Stars, Too; In Jacksonville, Several Homes Have Been in Films … and in Political Diplomacy," http://insurancenewsnet.com/oarticle/2013/11/20/houses-can-be-movie-stars-too-in-jacksonville-several-homes-have-been-in-fil-a-424938.html#.UpUGP7Cx5uE.

Interview List

Rick Ambrose, location manager

Janine Anzalone, *Exposure*, executive producer

Lisa Bradberry, Florida film historian

Tom Fallon, location manager/assistant director

Vishitra Garig, Clay County Archives, archives specialist

Mitch Harbeson, location manager

S. Bryan Hickox, The Paul Project, executive producer

Ron Kivett, author

Karrie Massee, Club Continental manager

Carl Post, former Clay Film Commissioner

Todd Roobin, Jacksonville Film Commission

Jaclyn Slaybaugh, Director, Clay County Tourism Division

Dan Solomon, *Exposure*, Director, Somantic Productions

Exterior view of WAPE's site located on Highway 17, south of Orange Park. Begun in 1958, WAPE quickly became one of the most popular AM stations in the southeastern U.S. (Courtesy of Barry Mishkind, OldRadioArchive.com.)

Radio Country Club: The Big WAPE

Michael Ray FitzGerald

Like many Orange Park High School teenagers, on warm weekends I would visit WAPE-AM's studios on Highway 17 in Fleming Island. The station had an unusual setup: you could swim in the pool, dive under the glass wall, and emerge in the lobby. From there you could see the "boss jocks" in action through a big glass window.

The "Big Ape" exploded into Northeast Florida in October 1958, quickly becoming the area's top-rated radio station. By the time my Navy family moved to the area, WAPE-AM was an institution.

The station was the fourth in a chain run by Bill Brennan, a Harvard-educated engineer with a thick Alabama twang who piloted his own plane between stations. It featured a blend of pop, country, and rhythm and blues, targeted at the burgeoning youth audience.[192]

[192] "Gone Ape," *Time*, Aug. 24, 1959, http://time.com/time/magazine/article/0,9171,864849,00.html. Interview with Tom Register, Feb. 28, 2010.

The WAPE pool served a dual purpose: a cooling pond for station equipment and a conventional swimming pool, attracting local teenagers on the weekends. (Courtesy of Barry Mishkind, OldRadioArchive.com.)

By shooting its signal along the coastline, WAPE could be heard all the way to Virginia Beach. Its 50,000-watt "blowtorch" was cooled by a water tank that fed a large, kidney-shaped swimming pool.[193] The station hosted pool parties on weekends, welcoming teenagers—especially bikini-clad girls.

Employees called it the "radio country club."[194] The offices included Brennan's private apartment with a full bar, state-of-the-art hifi, and mood lights that throbbed to the music. He could often be seen poolside, directing operations in swim trunks. As the Time article observed, "An outsider would have thought that Hugh Hefner had built a Playboy Mansion annex on U.S. 17."[195]

In Wilmington, N.C., a 23-year-old DJ at 1,000-watt WGNI, was listening to WAPE and decided it was time to move up to the big leagues. In 1963, he submitted a tape and was immediately hired. Sheldon Summerlin, or "Uncle Dino" as he dubbed himself, soon became the Big Ape's hottest talent.[196] His estranged father, Ben Outlaw, happened to live in Green Cove Springs, only a few miles from WAPE's studios.

Tom Register, the station's promotions manager at the time, says Summerlin's arrival was underwhelming. "When Dino first came to town, he was driving a 1947 DeSoto—a rusty, old hunk of junk." To augment his meager salary, he began emceeing weekend teen dances at Jacksonville's Northside Youth Center.[197]

---

[193] Mary Jo McTammany, "Clay Never the Same after the Big Ape," *Florida Times-Union*, Aug. 20, 1997.
[194] Ibid., "Gone Ape." See also, "WAPE Adopts Monkeyshines," *Billboard*, Nov. 24, 1958, 13.
[195] Ibid., "Gone Ape."
[196] Interview with Tom Register, Feb. 28, 2010.
[197] Ibid.

WAPE presented "record hops" hosted by its DJs. Owner Brennan expanded this into a series of concerts dubbed The Big Ape Shower of Stars, which brought in big-name acts eager to support the program in return for heavy airplay. The concert business was a logical extension of his radio operation: Big Ape's DJs would start hammering the acts' records weeks before the show, the increased exposure would guarantee packed halls, record sales would soar.[198] Brennan even brought the Beatles to Jacksonville. Hurricane Dora had hit the city the day before the concert, but the storm did not stop 23,000 Beatlemaniacs from flocking to the Gator Bowl.[199]

Register began promoting his own dances featuring the Lemon Twisters, fronted by "Little Robert" Moore, a flamboyant, young R&B singer who modeled his style on James Brown's and Jackie Wilson's.[200] He stapled posters to telephone poles near high schools.

Radio spots would have swallowed up his paltry budget, but he had a clever idea. He approached WAPE jocks Jack Mock and Cliff Hall Jr. and offered them $25 to make appearances at his dances. Register didn't care how long they performed—in fact, it didn't matter if they showed up at all, as long as they "talked up" their appearances on the air a few days before the show. Register offered Summerlin $5 more than he was making emceeing dances at the Northside Teen Center. Summerlin accepted and dutifully began plugging his upcoming appearances on his afternoon radio program.[201]

---

[198] "WAPE Adopts."

[199] Another 7,000 purchased tickets but could not make it because of road closings.

[200] Charlie Patton, "One of Jacksonville's Lemon Twisters Still Has a Little James Brown." *Florida Times-Union*. Oct. 8, 2009.

[201] Register interview.

When he saw how much Register was raking in, he demanded a share in the enterprise. He expanded their business model to include more acts and rotate them. Register would run the shows; Summerlin would entertain during breaks and handle promotion. They agreed to split the proceeds evenly.[202] Register recalls,

> I saw Dino take unknown bands and start pumping their records on the air, and Wham-O! By the time of the show, you would think they were a famous, worldwide act.[203]

Soon Summerlin was raking in 10 times more than the $85 he was making at WAPE. He formed his own label, which released records by acts he managed. Then he boosted them on the air. In an unparalleled act of brazenness, he recorded his own single and hammered it to the No. 1 spot on WAPE's "Top Five at Five."

Other jocks saw dollar signs and followed suit. If you had a band and wanted to get your music on the air, all you had to do was let a WAPE DJ manage you or sign you to his record label. Everyone seemed pleased with the results. Brennan was pleased because it was good promotion for the station. The bands were pleased because they were garnering airplay and packed houses.

The plan seemed perfect—except it was illegal. Summerlin's making money off acts whose records he was playing on-air was not only against FCC regulations, in some states it was considered commercial bribery, a misdemeanor punishable by a year in prison. This sort of thing had created a

[202] Ibid.
[203] Ibid.

massive scandal in 1960 when WABC New York DJ Alan Freed was fired for taking "payola."[204] Stations involved in such conflicts of interest could even lose their licenses. Worried owners began cleaning up their acts.

Bill Brennan didn't worry. Register suggests it might have been because he had close friends, former Harvard classmates, at the FCC.[205] Brennan turned a blind eye to Summerlin's shenanigans for several reasons, not least because he enjoyed having all those girls around.

"Dino was a chick magnet," Register says. "He made sure Bill was fixed up."[206]

Summerlin left in August 1965 to join rival WPDQ-AM, which pushed the Big Ape out of the top spot. Register left, too. The dance business was doing so well he didn't need the job anymore.

For the most part, things were squeaky-clean at 'PDQ, though Summerlin did manage to get his clients, the Dalton Gang's, records on the air. He and Register maintained their teen dance business and personal appearances on the side, but they paid for spots like any other ad clients—no more free plugs. "WPDQ had high standards," former news reporter Bill Greenwood explains. "It did not sponsor concerts and did not allow its DJs to promote their outside activities." Such practices

---

[204] Freed also deployed "kickback" schemes such as having himself listed as cowriter on certain songs. Philadelphia DJ Dick Clark took these schemes even further, owning equity in record labels whose records he played on his programs, plus publishing rights to certain songs, along with management commissions for certain acts. Fredric Dannen, *Hit Men: Power Brokers and Fast Money Inside the Music Business* (New York: Times Books, 1990), 46-47.

[205] Register interview.

[206] Ibid.

were common at other area stations, Greenwood adds.[207] Summerlin had his finger in every pie. Jacksonville television station WFGA (TV-12) got in on the action with an after-school music series called "Shakin' up Summer." Producer Virginia Atter Keys hired him to emcee. He installed the Dalton Gang as regulars. Big Ape jock Ken Fuller was the band's "key-boardist).[208] The Dalton Gang even wrote the show's theme song, which was released on Summerlin's label and played heavily on 'PDQ.

Thanks largely to the Big Ape, Jacksonville's music scene was booming. Musicians flocked from all over Florida and Georgia to get in on the action.[209]

Summerlin and Register finally had a falling out. Register estimated he'd been bilked out of about $18,000, due to Summerlin's skimming from the dance receipts. When confronted, Summerlin laughed and said it was just business, nothing personal. "I wanted to kick his ass," Register said.

About a year later, Register got a call from Summerlin in the wee hours. Bill Brennan had crashed his new Lear Jet carrying two passengers into a residential backyard near Herndon Airport outside Orlando.[210] Brennan's widow decided to sell the station.

---

[207] Email correspondence with Bill Greenwood, Feb. 10, 2011.
[208] Interview with Virginia Atter Keys, May 2001.
[209] Mack Doss, telephone interview, April 18, 2015. For a list of famous musicians who lived and performed in Jacksonville, see North Florida Music Hall of Fame, http://larrycohenproductions.com/N_Fla_Music.htm.
[210] National Transportation Safety Board, File 1-1120, NTSB identification no.: MIA68A0053, n.d.; email correspondence with Leroy Cumbie, Jan. 25, 2010.

There had been rumors and rumblings. The FCC finally undertook an investigation. The station was fined $9,000. Billboard reported in February 1970,

> The FCC says certain WAPE DJs accepted payments from dance promoters for the broadcast of announcements on the WAPE Dance Calendar. [An] investigation found that the payment for the DJ was disguised as a fee for his personal appearance. FCC also suspected conflict of interest in the fact that the station's chief, Ike Lee, selected music to be played over the station on the Dance Calendar program [while being paid to emcee the dances].[211]

This was merely a more elaborate version of the scheme Register had devised seven years before.

WAPE's new owners Stan and Sis Kaplan, who operated WAYS in Charlotte, cleaned house. The DJs who did so much to enrich the area's music scene—and themselves—were gone.

Teen dances began disappearing. It wasn't just the sudden dearth of radio promotion that killed them: the music was different, Register says. You couldn't dance to it. "Kids would sit on the floor and listen while the bands jammed." When the lights went dim, the joints came out: "It looked like some sort of candlelight vigil."

Register went to work at his father's plant nursery. Singer Little Robert left for South Florida, where he found brief success on T.K. Records with a group called Miami. Summerlin left WPDQ to become program director at tiny WWPF-AM in

---

[211] "WAPE fined $9,000 for Dance Promotion," *Billboard*, Feb. 28, 1970.

Palatka. After a few stints in Texas and Arkansas, he returned to his hometown, Asheville, where he became manager at WWNC, which he helped make the nation's top-rated country station.[212]

In 1986, he called Register, explaining he'd been saved and needed to atone. He gave Register $1,100 and died of heart failure the next week.[213]

---

212 Information about WWNC's ratings from Dan MacDonald, "Dino Summerlin Could Never Say No to Anyone," *Florida Times-Union*, July 5, 1986, B2.

213 Register interview. MacDonald, ibid., also mentions Summerlin's conversion.

Station management encouraged WAPE DJs to conceal their identities by wearing ape costumes when they worked. (Courtesy of Barry Mishkind, OldRadioArchive.com.)

A confluence of factors made Jacksonville a music city. The first was the southern tradition of storytelling and song. The second was the baby boom. The third, and the catalyst, was the addition of a massively powerful radio station, which, unlike major stations in other regions, did not shy away from playing records by local acts. Area musicians witnessed friends becoming famous overnight and were ignited by inspiration.[214]

Chains like Clear Channel and Cox Communications replaced freewheeling entrepreneurs like Bill Brennan. These chains could not risk the questionable practices of their predecessors. With radio support gone, the area's thriving music scene began to evaporate.

Ironically, it was those questionable practices that helped put Northeast Florida on the musical map. Without realizing it, local DJs and station owners helped create a vibrant music scene that would benefit the area for decades. Yet Register doubts there was any sense of altruism: "We were only trying to make a buck," he says. It was corrupt, he admits, but few if any of the participants recognized this. "We didn't feel we were doing anything wrong, and the ones who should have known better didn't give a damn."[215]

Selected Reference

Dannen, Fredric. Hit Men: Power Brokers and Fast Money Inside the Music Business. New York: Times Books, 1990.

[214] Dorothy Fletcher, "Radio Station WAPE Provided Soundtrack for Growing Up in Jacksonville," *Florida Times-Union*, Apr. 30, 2009, http://jacksonville.com/community/mandarin_sun/2009-04-23/story/radio_station_wape_provided_soundtrack_for_growing_up_in_jac.

[215] Interview, Register, May 27, 2011.

A popular local creature, the stuff of songs, myths, folklore, and celebrations since the 1980s, the Bardin Booger says, "Hello." (Courtesy of Lena Crain.)

The Bardin Booger Unmasked

Lena Crain

Most reports of the legendary Bardin Booger emerge from a little country town called Bardin, located on the outskirts of Palatka, just south of the Clay County line. Sightings of this Florida Bigfoot may date back to the early 1900s, though most started in the 1980s.[216] Whatever the facts, over the years I got to know the Bardin Booger well.

Witnesses describe him as big, black, hairy, and bad smelling. I talked to a lady who said the Booger[217] ran across the road in front of her car as she drove down Bardin Road. She said he stepped over the fence like it wasn't even there, but she was too scared to stop and investigate.

On April 28, 1981, after reading Jody Delzell's article in the *Palatka Daily News*, "The Booger Ventures too Close for Comfort," I suggested to my late husband, Billy Crain, that he write a song about him. Billy sat down and wrote it in about five minutes. The chorus of "Bardin Booger" goes like this:

> Every day you love to roam
> Running through the bushes and running
> through the trees.

---

[216] Whether this is the "beast" reportedly seen in the area of Jennings State Forest and Camp Blanding is not clear. Vishi Garig, "This Month in Clay County History," *Neighbor to Neighbor*, May 2016, 29.

[217] Booger is another word for bogeyman.

Mr. Bardin Booger, don't get me, please.
Hey, Mr. Bardin Booger your coat is black,
hairy on your face and hairy on your back.
When I see you, I get weak in the knees.
Mr. Bardin Booger, don't get me, please.[218]

At the time, Billy had a 30-minute radio show on local station WSUZ in Palatka. He played this song on his show, and the public started calling in and asking for the record, so we sent off the tape and had a 45-rpm record made. We sold quite a few copies of that song.

In 1982, Don Sports bought WSUZ and hired Billy to entertain at radio remotes to promote local businesses. We decided to take the Bardin Booger along to these events and came up with a costume for him. It was an instant hit with children and adults alike. All that time, we worked our day jobs. I was a shift supervisor at the Palatka Mill, and Billy was an auto mechanic and a good one.

Bud's Store in Bardin, is another focal point for the legend. For years, Bud kept the story alive, selling t-shirts and other Booger memorabilia, including Billy's record. Bud sold boxes of that record. I still have a few copies left, probably a collector's item by now.

---

[218] Written in 1981 and recorded by the late Billy Crain. Published by Billy and Lena's Publishing Company, BMI. Used with permission from Lena Crain, also known as the Bardin Booger.

Billy Crain, radio personality and country singer, with Lena Crain, celebrating New Year's Eve in a club near Green Cove Springs, circa 1980s. (Courtesy of Lena Crain.)

Although Bud died a few years back, plenty of people still stop by the store and ask about the Booger.

When writer Lillian Brown heard about the Booger, she invited me to make a presentation at her group, League of American Pen Women, in Palatka. I showed up in costume, and we have been great friends ever since and done guest appearances together many times.

Billy and I were always together when we weren't working. He passed away suddenly and too young, November 23, 1992, at age 53. I planned to retire the Booger then, but the public wouldn't stand for that. He still makes live appearances.

Lilly isn't the only writer fascinated by the Booger. I still get calls for interviews from around the region. Many of the *Palatka Daily News* articles were written by former publisher Jody Delzell. He wrote a book, *The Enigmatic Bardin Booger*, and invited the legendary Boog to his book signing. Long a staple of school visits, holiday festivals, and parades in Putnam, Clay, and surrounding counties, the Boog still gets around.

More Interest from the West Coast

Several years ago, I got a call from radio-talk-show host Rodney Bardin, who broadcasts from KCTY 107.7 in Long Beach, California. Some listeners called in and asked him if he was related to the Bardin Booger. Rodney asked a local librarian to try and locate the author of the "Bardin Booger" song. She tracked me down and asked permission to give Rodney my address.

He wrote and sent me $5 for a copy of the record. We've been friends ever since. Rodney has even tried to interest a movie company in making a film about the Booger. No luck yet.

Lillian Brown introducing the Bardin Booger before a program at the Shepherd's Center of Orange Park, May 2010. (Courtesy of Lena Crain.)

The Beat Goes On

People still listen to our songs. I released Billy's "Bardin Booger" on a compilation CD, and it has been played all over the world. So has one I wrote, "Bardin Booger's Christmas Wish," which Hilltop Records in Hollywood put to music. People still call me from time to time, hoping to book the "real" Booger—of course, those don't pan out.

Next time you drive down the pine-tree lined roads in southern Clay or northern Putnam County, keep a sharp eye on the woods. You might just catch a glimpse of that old Bardin Booger.

If you do, remember to wave.

Blondie, found by the St. Johns River, became a beloved pet and radio personality. (Courtesy of Lillian Kiernan Brown.)

A Tale of Friendship: Blondie and the Bardin Booger

Lillian Kiernan Brown

The Bardin Booger brought Lillian Brown and Lena Crain together. Their husbands, Jim Brown and Billy Crain, also became fast friends. The Bardin Booger and a little dog named Blondie completed the picture.

The Boog and Blondie developed a special relationship Lilly captured in a children's story she wrote a few years ago.

Christmas on the St. Johns River

My name is Blondie. I'm a Pomeranian-Spaniel mix, and I always have a smile on my face. Just ask my friends.

One chilly Christmas Eve, I was born in a lovely house on the St. Johns. The river flowed right past our door. The trouble was, my master did not want a mutt like me. When I was no more than six weeks old, he grabbed me by the scruff of my neck and threw me in the river. Freezing water swirled around me, pulling me under. What Scrooge would destroy a puppy's life like that? He didn't even give me a chance. I was so afraid.

Maybe it was an angel who called to the Bardin Booger as he roamed alongside the river looking for his Christmas dinner.

Whatever it was, I felt myself scooped up in a pair of strong, furry arms.

The Bardin Booger saved me in the depths of my crisis. His big black eyes gazed into mine, and I realized he gave me the gift of life. At that moment, I heard the most beautiful sound, a choir from the nearby church, singing "O Holy Night."

After the Booger rescued me, he carried me to Miss Lilly's doorstep. She took me in, dried me off, and warmed me gently with love and affection. Mr. Jim became my very dear friend, and I became his little Blondie, a place I held in his heart till the end.

Every Christmas Eve for 15 years, the Booger came to our door with the merriest Christmas wishes. Everybody joined in to sing "O Holy Night." and other songs. I sang right along with them.

And every year we rejoice in our friendship and pray for another year together in love. Because we have all learned that love is the finest gift of all. If you have love in your life, you have everything.

As I walk the banks of the St. Johns each Christmas with my loving master Mr. Jim, we are reminded that I, a little mutt of a dog, am a Christmas miracle, and the Bardin Booger is my guardian angel.

Bah humbug, I say, to all the Scrooges out there, and blessings to all the loving people all around the world. The Bardin Booger and my friends and family love me so, and unconditional love is what I return.

Before you move on, remember many mutts like me live right here in Clay County, and we're just waiting for a loving home. How about visiting a shelter near you? You might just find a bundle of love with your name on it. If so, you're lucky. When you give, you also receive.

Happily Ever After

The story behind the Christmas tale began in September 1999. Lilly Brown was teaching a creative writing class for children at the Larimer Arts Center in Palatka. During a break, her students went outside to play. They were surprised to find a little puppy on the banks of the St. Johns River, starving, frightened, wet, and dirty. Little did they know, this would be the start of a 17-year companionship.

Lilly took the puppy home, creating a family milestone. Blondie loved people, and she loved to sing with people. Everyone she met, in person or on the airwaves, quickly discovered what a good singing voice she had. "Happy Birthday" was her favorite song. Singing was just one of the little dog's brilliant ways of spreading life, love, and hope to others over the course of her life. She remained friendly and outgoing to the end of her days.

Along with Lena, Lilly, and the Bardin Booger, Blondie became a frequent guest on Rodney Bardin's radio talk show on KCTY in Long Beach, California. People often called in with requests for a song from Blondie. The quartet brought their own brand of joy and laughter to all who listened.

The Booger crew also performed on local radio shows. In 2012, listeners voted Blondie and the Bardin Booger "Mascots of WTCS Country Shoe Box Radio" in the little town of Gretna, Florida. When you have talent, word gets around.

Eventually, though, we all move on. Blondie was nearly 17 years old when she passed away. She took that journey as Miss Lilly held her close. Lilly and daughter Katherine Fries sang Blondie's favorite song as the little dog sighed for the final time. "Goodbye, for now, dear angel. We will meet again one day on the Rainbow Bridge."

Young Frank Towers trained at Camp Blanding. He returned to Florida following the war, eventually helping to establish a museum at the Camp and serving as a docent there for many years. (Courtesy of Frank Towers, Jr.)

Frank Towers: A Consequential Stranger

Beth Eifert

The people we love give our lives a sense of constancy and depth. Yet strangers can offer a needed disruption to old beliefs and help us view the world in new ways. This happened to me one cold February day a couple of years ago.

It was my daughter's eighteenth birthday. Family and friends gathered on the shore of Lake Kingsley at Camp Blanding to celebrate. Kathryn, the second of our two children, was a high school senior at the time. It was only a matter of months before she would join her older brother in college.

I watched nostalgically as she and her friends dared each other to take the polar bear plunge. If I squinted just enough, they looked like they could be 10 again, so I squinted a while longer, but soon felt the bittersweet wistfulness of trying desperately to hold on to what I knew I needed to release. I decided to get up and walk over to the little military museum on post that chronicles the history of the base.

I find history comforting. Stories told through time remind me of the universality of the human experience. They help me feel less-alone, especially when faced with life's challenges, so I walked over to the Camp Blanding Military Museum.

High school friends celebrate a birthday at Kingsley Lake, a nearly round lake located on the grounds of Camp Blanding. (Photo by Beth Eifert.)

As I climbed the brown wooden steps to the khaki-colored, clapboard building, I hoped I might find some comfort or wisdom from the stories of others who lived before me. Upon opening the door, I saw an elderly man and a middle-aged woman engaged in conversation.

The man looked about 80 years old, balding on top with wisps of white hair around the sides. He was tall and barrel-chested, with a calm, deep baritone voice. He wore a tan shirt with a name tag and looked up as I walked in.

"Welcome," he said.

"Thank you."

"Have you been to the museum before?"

"Yes, but it's been a while."

"Well then, welcome back, and let me know if you have any questions."

"Will do."

The man and woman resumed their talk, and I turned to look at the first exhibit of World War II artifacts. Amid the maps and war and military ribbons were myriad pictures of young men who had stepped away from the comfort of their homes and families to train along the shores of this very lake—over 800,000 men in all from 1940 through 1945. They were here to prepare for the horrors of what would be WWII.

They left behind 800,000 mothers. How did they cope? Where did they turn for wisdom?

In a scene meant to replicate daily camp life, a deck of playing cards was laid out, mid-hand, on a foot locker next to metal military-issued dishes, as if the players had been unexpectedly called away. A purple pillow with "Mother" stitched in bright yellow lay propped next to a neatly made wooden cot. Staring at the scene, I felt a lump welling in the back of my throat. It was interrupted by the conversation at the museum entrance.

The woman held the man's hand with both of her own. "This was wonderful, Frank, I can't thank you enough." She turned and headed toward the exit. As she started to go through the door, she paused and looked at me, "You really need to hear his story," and closed the door behind her. The man looked down to straighten a stack of brochures on a nearby table. His cheeks were red.

I had originally expected to tour the museum alone, but I now felt compelled to break the silence.

"My name's Beth," I said. I walked up the aisle to where the man was standing.

"I'm Frank Towers." We shook hands.

"Frank, it sounds like I need to hear your story."

He chuckled and shook his head, his cheeks reddening again. "I'm not sure it's all that special."

I got the sense that it was, and that he was ready to share. That he was meant to share it and I was meant to listen. I smiled and paused, hands clasped in front of me, and looked at Frank.

"Well," he said, "I trained here in 1941."

"You trained here? Wow, you look too young."

"I'm 97."

And with that, Frank started his fascinating story. "I was born on June 13, 1917, in Massachusetts and enlisted in the 43rd Infantry Division in 1940 when I was 23."

Frank said the 43rd Infantry Division consisted of the Vermont, Connecticut, Rhode Island, and Maine National Guards. Seventy-three years ago to the month—February 1941—

the United States Military called Frank and his fellow citizen soldiers into action and sent them to train at Camp Blanding.

"Twelve of us lived together in one of these tents for a full year," he said. He pointed to a vintage camp photo hanging on the wall. "We got to know each other very well."

At that time, they were training for a mission to the Pacific, but in late 1943, Frank's commander selected him to attend Officer Candidate School. Upon graduation, he transferred to the 120th Regiment, 30th Infantry Division as 1st Lieutenant Towers. There, he and his buddies yearned for their first deployment. Frank said, "We thought we could win this war and get it over with in a few months. Little did we know of the suffering to come in the years ahead."

In February 1944, they got their wish and shipped out to Europe. For the next few months, rumors about their mission were rampant as the men of the 30th Infantry trained in tactical maneuvers.

On June 6, D-Day, the thunder of the planes overhead confirmed the operation had begun. Frank and his unit landed on Omaha Beach in Normandy one week later, on his 27th birthday. Not part of the initial attack, they waded through its gruesome aftermath to face the enemy. "This was the biggest birthday reception I ever had, although not a joyful one."

For the next 282 days, the 30th Infantry Division experienced continuous combat in all the major battles in the European Theater of Operations. Fighting the German Elite 1st SS Division, they broke through the lines at St. Lo and again at Mortain, which allowed General Patton and his forces to race across France, likely shortening the war.

From northern France, they marched a staggering 25 to 50 miles per day to become the first Allied troops to enter

Belgium. In August, they helped to breach the Siegfried Line, a nearly 400-mile network of defensive structures throughout Germany. By September 12, Frank's division took Aachen, the first German city captured in WWII, and helped liberate Maastricht, the first Dutch town to be freed.

From mid-December till February, Frank's division fought in Belgium in the Battle of the Bulge and three months later came face to face with evidence of Hitler's final solution—the elimination of European Jews now called "the Holocaust." Frank said,

> Before we went into Germany, we were told about the concentration camps and about the torture these people had to endure, but we didn't believe it. We thought it was propaganda until we saw it firsthand.

On April 13, his unit moved into northern Germany near Magdeburg on the Elbe River, where they were told about an abandoned train to their east. When they arrived at the scene, they learned the train was filled with Jewish prisoners being transported from the Bergen-Belsen concentration camp, to the infamous Theresienstadt camp for extermination. Frank said,

> The cars were designed for 40 men or eight horses, but most of the 40 cars held up to 80 people. When the doors were opened, the stench from the waste and disease was unbearable.

There were 2,500 Jews inside. Some were already dead. All were deathly thin and covered with lice. Some had typhus. Frank said he and his men weren't sure at first what to do with them. "We were trained as soldiers, not on how to give humanitarian aid."

As a liaison officer, Frank knew the local roads well and was placed in charge of finding transportation for the survivors. He and his men relocated them to Hillersleben, a liberated German city with a hospital staffed by American medical teams. Afterward, Frank and his men left to continue fighting until the war ended in March of 1945.

Between 1946 and 1950, Frank worked as the Assistant Post Exchange Officer in Frankfurt, Germany, ensuring the PX was stocked with items that soldiers needed to live and work. There, his wife joined him and during that time they had three children, twin daughters and a son.

Frank left the military as a captain in 1950 and settled with his family near Gainesville, Florida. He operated a small grocery store there for 12 years, then worked at the University of Florida as an administrative assistant until he retired in 1979.

Around 2005, Frank discovered some notes he had written during his time at war, and he began to wonder what happened to the Holocaust survivors. Six hundred of those he helped save were children.

An internet search put him in touch with history teacher Matthew Rozell, who led a project with his students called "Teaching History Matters." Rozell and his students sought to uncover details behind a story they heard about a Nazi "death train."

Through Matthew, Frank was able to reach one survivor who put him in touch with others. Soon, more survivors contacted Frank with stories of their lives since the liberation. By age 97, Frank connected with 250 survivors through email, phone, and in person. They included doctors, engineers, lawyers,

Frank at the Camp Blanding Museum beside a painting presented to him in New York City by artist Sara Atzmon. Her painting commemorates the arrival of Frank and other American troops to liberate the death train. (Photo by Beth Eifert.) http://jacksonville.com/community/shorelines/2009-12-12/story/man_who_helped_saved_2_500_jews_during_the_holocaust_will_spe_0

businesspeople, and artists from all over the world. Sara Atzmon was seven years old when Frank and the other soldiers rescued her from the train. She is now a well-known artist living in Israel. At a reunion with Frank in New York several years ago, she gave him a painting showing the story of the train, which now hangs in the Camp Blanding Military Museum.

Another survivor, Gerd Klestadt of Luxemburg, was 12 when he was rescued. He and Frank met in France during the 70th-anniversary observance of D-Day. During their visit, Frank fell ill with symptoms that Klestadt recognized as a heart attack. In an incredible stroke of karma, Klestadt called for help and saved Frank's life.

Until 2015, Frank drove a 50-mile round trip from home near Gainesville to volunteer at the museum he helped found.

"What keeps you coming back after all these years, Frank?" I asked.

"These atrocities never should have happened," he said. "Maybe I can help make sure it never happens again."

We stood silently together for a moment, until I realized I had been gone from my daughter's party for over two hours. I needed to get back.

"Frank, I'm speechless. Thank you. How have I lived for 20 years in Clay County and never heard of you?"

He chuckled and looked down. "It was my pleasure." He shook my hand and, with a smile, he turned to welcome other patrons who had walked in during our talk.

As I walked out of the museum and down the brown wooden steps of the khaki-colored, clapboard building, I realized I found the wisdom I had craved when I had walked in. Rather than coming from an inanimate exhibit, it came in the form of a hero living in my own community, whom I might never have met had I not meandered over to the museum.

Karen Fingerman, a professor at Purdue University, referred to such people as "consequential strangers," the peripheral connections we make each day who often have surprising and unexpected effects on our lives.

To me, Frank Towers was a consequential stranger. He helped me view my experiences through the broader spectrum of time. Smiling, I jogged back to the lake.

Epilogue: "Lest We Forget"

Frank Towers died July 4, 2016, at 99 years of life. When he died, people all over the world paused to remember his stories and recognize his contributions. Newspapers as diverse as the *National Catholic Register* in the United States and the Israeli newspaper *Haaretz* memorialized his passing.[219]

---

[219] Jerri Donohue, "Saving Souls on a Nazi Death Train: A Catholic veteran dedicates his final years to Holocaust education," *National Catholic Register* blog, July 22, 2016. http://ncregister.com/blog/jdonohue/saving-souls-on-a-nazi-death-train. Ofer Aderet, "U.S. Soldier Frank Towers, Who Rescued 2,500 Jews at End of WWII, Dies at 99," *Haaretz*, July 24, 2016. http://haaretz.com/world-news/europe/.premium-1.732761.

Frank with Marie-Therese Lavielle during one of his many visits to France to recall the past, recognize his fallen comrades and keep the memories alive. (Courtesy of Frank Towers, Jr.)

After the war, Frank worked tirelessly to preserve the memory of his fallen comrades and their struggle to protect our freedom, and to preserve the memory of the Holocaust. Award-winning high school history teacher Matthew A. Rozell focused on these experiences in his blog, "Teaching History Matters," and in several books including, *A Train Near Magdeburg: A Teacher's Journey into the Holocaust, and the Reuniting of the Survivors and Liberators.*[220]

Audiences throughout North America, Northern Europe, and Israel sought Frank out to learn from his stories. His humble, quietly impassioned style made his memories all the more compelling. As national president and executive secretary of the 30th Infantry Division Veterans of World War II Association, he led tours to Normandy for veterans of the 30th and their families, and he frequently visited on his own.[221]

"In June 1983, three American veterans of WWII stopped in the little community of Saint-Jean-de-Daye, the first city their Division liberated in 1944," said Saint-Jean-de-Daye resident Marie-Therese Lavieille, whom I met online after Frank's passing. "Among them was Frank Towers…. My husband and I invited them to dinner. That was the beginning of our long friendship."[222]

In 1984, Frank and 300 infantry veterans and their families revisited Saint-Jean-de-Daye and its cemeteries at Colleville-sur-Mer and Saint James, where many of their comrades were laid to rest. Frank returned several times over the years, staying with Marie and her husband, Claude.

---

[220] https://teachinghistorymatters.com/get-the-book-here/.

[221] Randy Lefko, "Army Major Pushes for Return of WWII Veterans," *Clay Today*, June 1, 2016. http://claytodayonline.com/stories/army-major-pushes-for-return-of-wwii-veterans,2512.

[222] Personal email from Marie-Therese Lavieille, Sept. 6, 2016.

(Upper) Frank with Hedva Perahia in Rehovot, Israel. Her mother Flora Gattegno was among those freed from the Falsleben train. *(Lower)* "Hommage a Frank Towers" honors Frank after his death. As World War II veterans aged and the trip to France became more difficult, Frank and Claude Lavielle formed Les Fleurs de la Memoire. Its members commit to continue laying flowers on the graves of American soldiers in *St. James, Normandy, and Colleville-sur-Mer. Ph*oto at Saint-Jean-de-Daye, Sept. 11, 2016. (Courtesy of Frank Towers, Jr.) http://lesfleursdelamemoire.com/en/association/objectifs

In 1990, Frank helped found Camp Blanding Military Museum, and until 2016, he volunteered there as a docent, retelling the stories of his war experiences.[223]

In 1994, Queen Beatrix of the Netherlands presented Frank with the Order of Orange-Nassau for the good will he promoted over the years between the United States and the Netherlands. Frank was the only non-Dutch person ever to receive this prestigious award.[224]

In 2000, Frank told his friends, the Lavieilles, “I’m getting old now, and soon I won’t be able to visit my comrades entombed here. How can we make sure they are not forgotten?”

With Frank’s support, Claude founded *Les Fleurs de la Memoire* (The Flowers of Memory), a group dedicated to caring for the graves of Americans buried in France and Belgium. To date, more than 14,000 graves have been adopted, with about 600 remaining.[225]

In 2009, French President Nicolas Sarkozy honored Frank with the French Legion of Honor Knightship for his lifelong pursuit of peace and friendship between our countries.[226]

On September 11th, 2016, the people of Saint-Jean-de-Daye, France, held a memorial service for Frank.

In Holland, members of the famous musical Rieu family hosted a gathering in Frank’s memory at the World War II Netherlands American Cemetery and Memorial in Margraten. A memory book encouraged visitors to share their memories of Frank or other “American Liberators.”

---

[223] Find more information on the 30th Infantry and Camp Blanding at: http://30thinfantry.org/blanding.shtml, including Frank’s personal account, “The Death Train at Farsleben Germany, April 13, 1945.”
[224] Lefko, “Army Major.”
[225] Ibid.
[226] Ibid.

Hedva Perahia met Frank in Israel in 2011. Her mother was one of the people on the train he helped liberate. In an online guestbook, she described Frank as "a human when humanity was insane. When he came to speak with us in Rehovot [Israel], he pointed to the people and said, "You are the real heroes because you survive."[227]

On July 8, 2016, Frank was buried in Forest Meadows Cemetery in Gainesville, Florida. He dedicated years of his life to educating others about the WWII, the train, and its survivors to underscore our shared humanity. Three words guided his commitment: "Lest we forget."

Selected References

Fingerman, Karen. "Consequential Strangers and Peripheral Ties: The Importance of Unimportant Relationships." *Journal of Family Theory & Review*, 1 June 2009: 69. https://researchgate.net/profile/Karen_Fingerman/publication/227902667_Consequential_Strangers_and_Peripheral_Ties_The_Importance_of_Unimportant_Relationships/links/0c96052bda04b4285b000000.pdf.

Haas, Darrin. "Still Shocking," *National Guard Magazine*, 2012. http://nationalguardmagazine.com/publication/?i=128954&p=40.

[227] http://legacy.com/obituaries/name/frank-towers-obituary?pid=100000180584812&page=5.

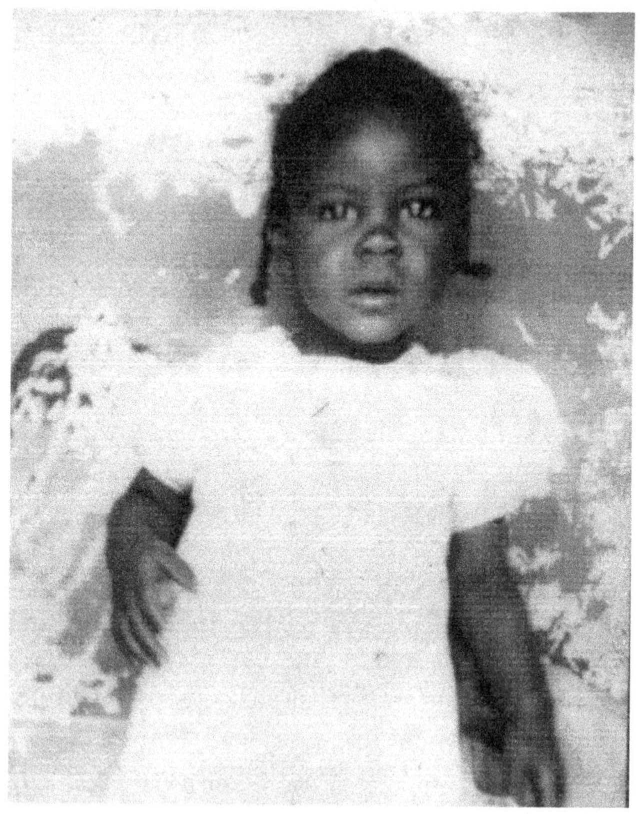

Young Maude Burroughs, about five years old. A family picture circa 1947. (Courtesy of Clay County Archives.)

A Life on Hill Top: Restoring a Community of Hope

Maureen A. Jung

A Daughter of Clay

> Middleburg is my birthplace. My history begins here and my education. Inasmuch as this is my beginning, I have the right, the obligation, and the responsibility to pass this heritage down to my children and the community. Some people may be afraid to look back and remember the past. I am not.[228]

Maude Burroughs Jackson was born in a turpentine camp beside Black Creek and grew up in Hill Top, a segregated rural community. As a college student, she participated in St. Augustine's civil rights struggle during the early 1960s. Following graduation, she taught elementary school in the Miami area and earned a master's degree in early childhood education. In 1994, after injuries from a car accident led her to retire early,

---

[228] Interview with Maude Burroughs Jackson. This and subsequent quotes from Maude come from a series of in-person and phone meetings October 2016 through March 2017.

Maude returned home to heal. Since then, she has worked tirelessly to discover and preserve Hill Top's history.[229]

It hasn't been easy. Little about life in Clay County's black communities was ever written down. Recognizing how easily this past could slip away, in 1995 Maude and other residents formed Hill Top Heritage Development, Inc. Their mission is "to undertake projects that restore hope, promote education, and foster self-reliance, self-respect, and self-love while rebuilding and further developing the community."[230] They set out to find and tell the stories of their past.

The Call of the Pines

Land grants and the area's cedar and first-growth pines attracted European colonizers to this area. Some brought enslaved Africans to carve plantations from the wilderness and swampland and plant indigo, cotton, and orange trees. Slaves played a significant role in one of the local economy's most valuable products: turpentine. They drained the trees to produce pitch and "naval stores" for the wooden ships plying an expanding sea trade.[231] It was brutal physical labor under relentless heat.

Following the Civil War, life for newly freed blacks improved little. Jim Crow laws throughout the South left them vulnerable to violence and intimidation. With nothing to bind them to the land, many families took to the road. Some struck out for northern cities; others headed south to Florida.

---

[229] "Old School House Moved," *Clay County Leader*, Sept. 21-28, 1995, 11.

[230] "Keeping Our Heritage Alive for All to Enjoy, The Rich Black History of Middleburg in Clay County, Florida," Hill Top Heritage Development, n.d., 8.

[231] Robert N. Lauriault, *"From Can't to Can't:* The North Florida Turpentine Camps, 1900-1950." *Florida Historical Quarterly,* 67 (Jan. 1989): 310-28.

Black families who arrived in Middleburg in the 1880s and '90s found hope in short supply, but some found jobs, mostly in turpentine camps. Camp owners rented shanties or shotgun shacks to workers and their families in the "quarters."

> We came by way of boats and ferries through Black Creek. We came from Georgia and South Carolina. We lived in small houses ... wood-framed, unpainted structures with wooden windows. Alongside the houses, you would often see small gardens with greens, okra, peas, corn, tomatoes, and potatoes.... In the backyard ... hogs, chickens, ducks, and a turkey or two.[232]

In 1868, Grant S. Forman made this journey from Barnwell, South Carolina, where he was born. Although he grew up near the plantation where his parents had been enslaved, in the late 1880s, the family left to find a better place.[233] A self-taught man, Forman's work ethic and unshakable faith earned him a reputation among blacks and whites alike for wisdom, generosity, and integrity. As he labored in Middleburg's turpentine camps, he dreamed of owning land, a place to feel safe, a home.[234]

The Federal Homestead Act allowed blacks as well as whites to apply for 160 acres of "free" land. To be eligible, the Act required homesteaders to clear and continuously improve their property for seven years. Some African Americans homesteaded in Clay, Forman among them. He applied for 161

---

[232] "Celebrating Over 100 Years of Our Community," (Middleburg, Fla.: Hill Top Heritage Development, Inc., 2003), 21.
[233] Anthony L. Thompson, "African American Families," typescript, n.d., 1.
[234] Ibid., 29.

acres in 1895 and went to work on improvements. He cut trees for pulpwood, planted crops, built a home, and eventually mined a clay deposit on his land—and he prospered. Those were good times—hard, but good—for a while.

In Clay, as throughout the South, some whites steadfastly opposed land ownership by blacks. Jim Crow laws were still firmly enforced. Violence could occur suddenly, and perpetrators had little reason to fear repercussions.[235] Stories handed down by older Hill Top residents alluded to an event said to have taken place in 1905: a white mob swarmed Hill Top in a violent attack.[236] Forman and the other residents fled as a group "in fear for their lives"—a community erased.[237]

Forman escaped to South Carolina; the others scattered to places unknown. Before leaving, he arranged to mail his annual property taxes of $4 to Frosard Buddington. The Middleburg businessman agreed to pay them, enabling Forman to keep the land until he felt safe to return.[238] Finding work on the railroad, he sometimes revisited this area to check on his property on the hill.

In 1919, he married Estelle Johnson, a widow with two children. Together they had 10 more children, though only four lived to adulthood.[239]

---

[235] See for example, the story of the Tutson family in 1871, "This brutal act came about basically because these white men wanted Tutson's land.... It is quite probable that other attacks of this nature occurred during these years but went unrecorded." Arch Fredric Blakey, *Parade of Memories: A History of Clay County, Florida* (Green Cove Springs, Fla.: Clay County Board of Commissioners, 1995), 102-103.
[236] "Keeping Our Heritage," 4.
[237] "Celebrating Over 100 Years," 29.
[238] "African American Families," 3.
[239] Ibid., 5.

The family got by until an accident left Forman unable to work for three years. He fell behind on his Florida taxes, though as his health improved, he resumed payments.

In 1936, amid the Great Depression, Forman moved his family back to Clay. By then, the elder Buddington had died. Due to the missing taxes, Buddington's son claimed half of Forman's land.

The wood-frame house Edd James Burroughs built by hand with help from his son Eddy during the 1940s. (Photo by Jack Rhyne.)

Return to the Hill

Disappointment didn't stop Grant Forman. Aiming to settle and rebuild, he eventually sold off parts of his remaining 80 acres to buyers, black and white. His generosity made it possible for Hill Top to grow. Together, they built a community forged in love, faith, and family.

Edd James Burroughs was among those who bought land in the growing black community. He had moved to Florida in 1926, bringing his wife Lena, son Edd, and other family members. They traveled from South Carolina, Alabama, and Georgia to find land to homestead. Initially, they settled in Russell, today part of Fleming Island, and worked for a timber operation.

Good with his hands, Edd James was soon known as one of the best workers in the turpentine camps. After working a while at Howard's quarters along Black Creek, he landed a better position and a larger house at Buddington's quarters, near where Middleburg Elementary School now stands. In 1942, that cabin in the turpentine quarters was where Maude was born.

Despite meager pay, Edd James managed to put money aside. He supplemented his income during the slow season, traveling to the Kissimmee area to join his relatives harvesting the citrus crop. In 1944, he and young Edd bought 10 acres of land, one portion from Forman and another from a white family named Walls. The Burroughs family moved up the hill, cut trees, cleared underbrush, planted a garden, and built a house. That house still stands.

Founding a Community

After Forman came back to Clay with his family to rebuild, other families followed him up the hill. He sold off parts of his remaining land to blacks and whites alike, including the Burroughs family. Maude's father, Edd James Burroughs, supplemented his income from the turpentine camp during the slow season, traveling to the Kissimmee area to join his relatives harvesting the citrus crop.

In 1944, he and his son bought 10 acres of Hill Top land, one portion from Forman and another from a white family named Walls. They moved up the hill, prepared the land, planted a garden, and built a house that still stands. Maude explained,

> That's the house I grew up in. My dad built that house. He cut the trees. He made the beams and stilts, and everything that went into it, using a few simple tools. When we moved here, others did too. Blacks became homeowners and landowners.

Grant Forman and the other new Hill Top residents believed in self-reliance and self-sufficiency. Like them, Edd James Burroughs worked as his own boss, cutting and selling lumber grown on his property. He also believed in home ownership, often telling the children, "Own your house, do not rent; even if you have to live in a matchbox, let it be your matchbox."

When her parents separated a few years later, the children stayed with their father. Their mother moved to Jacksonville, where they visited often. "Daddy took very, very, very good care of the five or six of us still at home. My baby sister, Lena, and I were the youngest," Maude said. When there was work to do, everybody worked. "At an early age, I knew how to cook and clean. I learned to help others."

At age nine, Maude found her first job. For three dollars a week, she washed and ironed a white man's clothes. "Three pairs of slacks, three pairs of socks, three undershirts, three shirts, all done in a washtub." She made good use of that money. "I bought my first new book, a Little Golden Reader, 39 cents. I also bought my first Christmas skirt, new socks, and black shoes. We only had the simple things, but we were taught to respect and appreciate life."

She recalls waking to her father playing the guitar and singing funny songs to get them out of bed in the morning before school. Everyone loved and joined in those songs. The house was filled with laughter, Maude said. "Whatever happened in life, nothing has been able to destroy the unity and love in our family. On Burroughs Road, you can still feel that love and concern."

"Founded on Faith and Kept by Love"

Middleburg's black families often relied on their belief in God to keep going. Many had little else. In 1904, they organized St. Mark Missionary Baptist Church. They met in a wood-framed building underneath towering oak trees near the present location of Middleburg Elementary School. St. Mark quickly became a focal point of the community.

After many families moved up the hill, congregation members walked or drove a wagon back down to attend services. Middleburg resident and former state representative Sam Saunders watched them make the long trek to and from the church.

He decided he could help. He donated a plot of land he owned in Hill Top as a new home for St. Mark. On that land, the residents came together to build a sturdy cement-block church, completed in 1956. Once again, faith created a lifeline in the community.

Middleburg Colored School, the only choice for local black children for 60 years. Today, the Black Heritage Museum helps preserve the memorabilia, photos, and stories of a difficult age. (Photo by Jack Rhyne.)

Back in the day, Maude said,

> Everybody came to the Christmas Eve program. The church used to get something for every one of the children in Hill Top. An apple or orange, candy, nuts, something to say "We are family. We love you, Merry Christmas." That love is the greatest gift of all. But it is a gift.

Today, more than 60 years later, the connections unwind as the population diminishes. Maude still attends St. Mark, along with her sisters Lena and Annie Lee, the last of their generation of the Burroughs family.

A School Apart

Along with the other children of Hill Top, all nine Burroughs children attended Middleburg Colored School, a one-room schoolhouse located across the street from Middleburg Elementary. Founded circa 1903, it was the only local school for blacks in the town until the 1967. Until the 1950s, it lacked both lights and plumbing. A single teacher taught first through ninth grades in one room.

During the week, the Hill Top children walked to and from school, a five-mile round trip. Most carried greasy lunch bags of biscuits, cornbread, or whatever was left from supper the night before. On cold days, they ran through the trees gathering fuel for the school's wood burning stove. When the Middleburg Elementary school bus drove slowly by on Highway 21, students on the bus often spit and shouted "Nigger" out the window at Maude and the other black students.

Edd Burroughs had prepared his children. “Always believe in God and yourself,” he told them. “A nigger is a low-down, dirty person. That is not you.” So, says Maude, the words rolled off their backs, especially once they got inside that little schoolhouse.

By state law, schools were both separate and unequal. Educational materials were discards from white schools.[240] Maude recalled what it was like:

> We didn’t have many books. Now and then we got a chance to share a book from Middleburg Elementary School after some pages had been torn out or written through. It might have been a mess, but it was a book. You learned whatever way you could.

And learn they did. Many went on to attend the segregated Paul Laurence Dunbar High School in Green Cove Springs, then on to one of the historically black colleges to become teachers, ministers, nurses, professors, and other community leaders. Dunbar graduates credit their teachers and lessons for much of this success. Maude said one poem she learned at Dunbar shaped her whole life.

---

[240] Bruce Vacca, “One-room Schools Still Stand,” *Clay Today*, Feb. 13, 1991, 9A.

The view from the Black Heritage Museum, overlooking the Hunter-Douglas Park in Hill Top. Maude Burroughs Jackson has motivated and inspired people young and old to ask questions and learn more about black history in Clay County. (Photo by Jack Rhyne.)

Myself[241]

Edward Guest

I have to live with myself and so
I want to be fit for myself to know.
I want to be able as days go by,
always to look myself straight in the eye;
I don't want to stand with the setting sun
and hate myself for the things I have done.

I don't want to keep on a closet shelf
a lot of secrets about myself
and fool myself as I come and go
into thinking no one else will ever know
the kind of person I really am,
I don't want to dress up myself in sham.

I want to go out with my head erect
I want to deserve all men's respect;
but here in the struggle for fame and wealth
I want to be able to like myself.
I don't want to look at myself and know
I am bluster and bluff and empty show.

I never can hide myself from me;
I see what others may never see;
I know what others may never know,
I never can fool myself and so,
whatever happens, I want to be
self-respecting and conscience free.

---

[241] This poem is in the public domain.

Dunbar High operated until 1967, when desegregation arrived in Clay. The school lives on in the memories and hearts of former students who still gather every two years to recall and celebrate the past they shared.[242] They grew up during an era already losing ground to time.

Vanishing Point

"Much of black history is contained in a rich oral tradition, which is more vulnerable to loss than the written word," Mary Jo McTammany wrote. She noted that in the 1930s, Clay County "was dotted with small one-room schools for blacks."[243]

Hill Top was just one of Clay's segregated black communities. Yet the few local history books say little about the experience and contributions of blacks in this area for over 200 years.

Even official records, if available, may omit essential parts of local history. For example, *Who's Who Politically Speaking in Clay County, Florida, 1958-1986* includes only white schools and those formed after desegregation in a list of "current and early schools."[244] Even the celebrated Dunbar High failed to make the list.

---

[242] Ulysses Pollard, editor, "A Memory Book of the Dunbar High School Reunion 2000," compiled under the supervision of the former teachers and staff of Dunbar High.

[243] "Black History Adds Depth and Richness to the Community's Story," *Clay Today*, Feb. 21, 2003.

[244] Compiled by the Research Committee of the Clay County Historical Commission, 1986.

A Community Lives on Within Us

Now in her '70s, Maude still shares her stories because she believes those who forget the past are bound to repeat it. "I can see that happening again." She continued,

To get a handle on life, we need to know our background. We went through so much; it didn't break us, it made us stronger. When you think where we came from, how far we have come, and how much more we could be doing, it takes my mind back to our beginnings. So much love and concern in the hearts of our fore-parents who worked together to build and save this community.

> Those memories keep Maude reaching out to tell "who we are and how we have been connected." The question, she says, is this: "How then shall we grow?"

Today the former Middleburg Colored School sits in Hill Top's Hunter-Douglas Park, named for two beloved elementary school teachers, Etta Douglas and Alice E. Hunter. The restored schoolhouse reopened as the Black Heritage Museum. Throughout the year, events at the Museum offer glimpses into the lives of those who carved out the community on the hill.

Selected References

Blakey, Arch Fredric, with an update by Bonita Thomas Deaton. *Parade of Memories: A History of Clay County, Florida.* Green Cove Springs, Fla.: Clay County Bicentennial Steering Committee, 1995.

Clay County Historical Commission. *Who's Who Politically Speaking in Clay County, Florida, 1858-1986*, Green Cove Springs, Fla: Board of County Commissioners, 1986.

"Keeping Our Heritage Alive for All to Enjoy, The Rich Black History of Middleburg in Clay County, Florida." Middleburg, Fla.: Hill Top Heritage Development, n.d.

Pollard, Ulysses, ed., "*A Memory Book of the Dunbar High School Reunion 2000.*" Green Cove Springs, Fla. 2000.

Today's Sunrise," March 11, 2017. Dawn lights boats on the St. Johns River and reaches out to Spring Park in Green Cove Springs. (Photo by Wanda Glennon Canady.)

Clay Today

Lynn Skapyak Harlin

Clay today is paved six-lane roads
instead of farms, fields and acres
of pine trees.
Now there are strip malls,
giant super stores, restaurants,
and fast food drive-thru
stops to tempt the passerby.
They crowd the county,
surrounded by black paved parking
spaces. Suburban sprawl spreads, one
Gated Community melding into
another, mile after mile,
houses too close to each other.
Yet neighbors often don't
know one another.
The pace is faster, more frenetic
people rush in shiny cars,
clogging roadways causing frustration.
The St. Johns River the only constant
always there yet flowing, going
steady north.

Contributing Writers

Maureen A. Jung, Ph.D., project director

Maureen has facilitated writing workshops for over 30 years, starting during graduate school at the University of California, Santa Barbara (UCSB). Her first professional publication appeared in 1981. A Fellow of UCSB's affiliate of the National Writing Project, the Society of American Archivists recognized her work on mining history with the Theodore Calvin Pease award. Maureen's article "Capitalism Comes to the Diggings," is an invited chapter in California's 150th-anniversary publication. She's written two White House presentations and a $15 million federal grant proposal, as well as dozens of articles and presentations. Working with contributors and supporters of this project over the past five years has taught her the meaning of "embedded in Clay."

Lynn Skapyak Harlin, editor

Poet, writer, and editor, Lynn Skapyak Harlin led the Shantyboat Writers Workshops for more than 16 years. She has edited scores of manuscripts, fiction and nonfiction. Recently she worked on portrait artist Ann Manry Kenyon's coffee table book, *Memories, Method and Mastery*. The book chronicles Kenyon's life and includes images of 100 of her paintings. For three years, with Carolee Bertisch and Sharon Scholl, Lynn led a poetry workshop at the Florida Heritage Book Festival. She has supported local poetry venues since the 1960s. Her first published poem "War Waste" appeared in *Time* magazine, in 1970. Her poems appeared in *State Street Review*, *Arbus*, *Section Eight Magazine*, *Florida Speaks*, *Aquarian*, *AC PAPA* (Ancient City Poets, Authors, Photographers and Authors), deadpaper.org, and ashandbones.com. Her chap books, *Real Women Drive Trucks* and *Press One for More Options* were published in 1997, and *Age Changes* in 2017.

Lillian Kiernan Brown

At age 14, Lily followed her mother into the glittering and shady world of Burlesque. As Lily Ann Rose, she worked with top entertainers of the time and attracted a devoted following until a wardrobe *faux pas* brought her career to an abrupt end. After being banned in Boston, Lily built a career as a journalist and radio personality, including working for the Armed Forces newspaper and Armed Forces radio in Morocco. At age 84, she's written a column for *Palatka Daily News,* for more than 20 years. Her story of Blondie and the Bardin Booger is in part a tribute to her late husband, Jim, and their beloved dog, Blondie, as well as to her friendship with Lena Crain, who carried on the Booger tradition.

Lena Crain

Billy and Lena Crain were married in 1975. Billy sang and played flat-top guitar; he wrote songs too. Billy always said he wanted to leave something behind to be remembered by, and Lena encouraged him to pursue a career in music. The two latched on to the story of the Bardin Booger in the early 1980s and built it into a tiny empire. Billy wrote and recorded "The Bardin Booger" in Nashville, and Lena still gets requests for the song. As the Bardin Booger, Lena has visited schools, conferences, parades, and other events, always portraying the kindly nature of the local Big Foot.

Beth Eifert

Beth's passion for people and their stories shows in everything she does. In 1996, she and her husband, Jim, moved to Clay County where they raised their two children, Austin and Kathryn. They stayed in Clay for nearly 20 years. Her natural fondness for and interest in the military springs from 30+ years as a military spouse and daughter of a World War II veteran. During a trip to Camp Blanding's military museum, just before her younger child left for college, Beth met one of its founders, the late Frank Towers, also a WWII veteran. His story inspired her during a time when she was most in need of a new perspective. Her essay about Frank marks Beth's inaugural participation in an anthology.

Michael Ray FitzGerald, Ph.D.

A film/television historian and a freelance journalist, Michael earned a bachelor's in journalism from Jacksonville University, a master's in mass communication from the University of Florida, where he taught journalism, and a doctorate in film and media studies from University of Reading (UK). He teaches communication at Flagler College and the University of North Florida. His book *Native Americans on Network TV* is a top seller in Rowman & Littlefield's *Film & History* line.

Tim Gilmore, Ph.D.

Author of 14 books including *Devil in the Baptist Church: Bob Gray's Unholy Trinity, Central Georgia Schizophrenia, The Mad Atlas of Virginia King, In Search of Eartha White,* and *Stalking Ottis Toole: A Southern Gothic.* His website, jaxpsychogeo.com, contains over 600 of his stories about significant and strange locations around Jacksonville.

Gilmore is the organizer of the Jax-by-Jax Literary Arts Festival and the Jax-by-Jax Reading Series. He earned his Ph.D. in English from the University of Florida and teaches composition and literature at Florida State College at Jacksonville.

Paula R. Hilton

Originally from New Castle, Pennsylvania, Paula earned her bachelor's degree in English from the University of Pittsburgh and an MFA from the University of New Orleans. Her fiction, essays, and poetry have appeared on NPR's *This I Believe*, as well as in literary journals, including *The Tulane Review*, *Kalliope*, and *Ellipsis*. Hilton's debut novel, *Little Miss Chaos*, recently received the *Kirkus* star for books of exceptional merit. The novel was also a short-listed finalist in the 2014 William Faulkner-William Wisdom Creative Writing Competition. She is currently working on *Daphne and the Delirious Girls*, her second book for young adults.

Inez Holger

Inez's love of writing wound its way through years of raising her family, caregiving, and volunteer work with the elderly and children. Her essay, "Origin of Fear," was nominated for the Pushcart Prize and named a Notable Essay in *Best American Essays 2011*. Her work has appeared in magazines, literary journals, online sites, and anthologies including *Bird in the Hand, Risk and Flight*, and *Easy to Love but Hard to Raise: Real Parents, Challenging Kids, True Stories*. Though she lives in Duval County, her husband's extended family lives in Fleming Island and has hosted an annual family reunion each Thanksgiving for decades. A short film made on their property inspired her choice for the Clay anthology.

Marshall Lenne

A retired human resources professional, Marshall spent 35 years observing, analyzing, and affecting human behavior. Educated in parochial schools, he received a Congressional Appointment to the United States Air Force Academy. After he received his degree and commission, he married and entered pilot training. Rated as USAF Instructor Pilot, Marshall was intimately involved in motivating and training pilots to make the right decisions under stress. After completing his USAF service, Marshall entered civilian life and the field of human resources. Marshall and his wife live in Green Cove Springs, Florida. They have two daughters and three grandchildren.

Nancy Moore

Born in 1941 in Cleveland, Ohio, Nancy majored in communications at Cedarville University. Graduate courses at University of Massachusetts and Otterbein College furthered her fascination with language, written and spoken. She taught English and public speaking, tutored ESL students, worked as an educational therapist, and applied her English skills in business. At Penney Farms Retirement Community, Nancy chairs the Penney Writers group and co-edits *Penney for Your Thoughts*, a monthly newsletter. She has edited and written several editions of *Spotlight on the 90's*, biographical sketches of retirees in their 90th decade. She compiled and wrote the 90th anniversary edition of the expanded Penney Farms history, *Dreams and Legacies* (2017), which contains interviews with residents, town officials, staff, and board members.

Bryan Joseph Pitchford

Born in Annapolis, Maryland, to a military family, Bryan is now a Major in the Florida Army National Guard. He's served in the United States military for over 18 years, including three deployments to the Middle East. Bryan recently earned a master of fine arts in creative writing from National University. He poems have appeared in Saint Leo University's The Sandhill Review (2003 and 2004), Florida State Poets Association Anthology Thirty (2012), The Desert Mesh (2013), and Along the Forgotten Coast: Big Bend Poets' Anthology (2014).

Diane E. Shepard

Moving to the slower pace of Clay County proved a wellspring for Diane's creativity. Both her children and her writing career were born here. A poet, writer, columnist, and copy editor, Diane's written work has appeared in many publications, including *Word Trips* (Hidden Owl Books, 2007), *Open Mic Jacksonville, Vol. II, Clay Today* newspaper, and *Our Town* magazine. Her daughter's enchanting sketches punctuate Diane's current labor of love, *Keeping Time with Turtles and Other Lessons from My Children*, a collection of columns and poems. Relationships with her family and her writing career in Clay County nourish Diane's creative spirit.

Joan T. Warren

A pediatric occupational therapist and aspiring writer in Clay County, Joan's work includes a curriculum project for addiction recovery and three blogs, with other projects in progress. She enjoys discovering inspirational life experiences, past and present. She hopes her writing leaves a trail for future generations to find greater wholeness and health from the inside out.

Image Credits

Courtesy of Clay County Archives

Flora and fauna on Black Creek
Fishing along Black Creek
Infantry training, Camp Blanding
Artist's interpretation, Laurel Grove Plantation
Penelope Borden Hamilton
Young Augusta Christine Fells
The Harp (2 views)
Yale Primate Research Facility, fence
Robert Yerkes, two chimpanzees
Ice plant, Green Cove Springs
Coke delivery truck
Grady Smith
Clay County Council on Aging
Colonial Inn (2 views)
Zaat poster
Young Maude Burroughs

Courtesy of City of Jacksonville, Jacksonville Public Library

Unnamed sculpture, Augusta Savage

Courtesy of Barry Mishkind, OldRadioArchive.com

Exterior view of WAPE's site
WAPE pool
WAPE DJ in ape suit

Courtesy of the State Archives of Florida

The Clark-Chalker House, Middleburg
Soil testing at Shadowlawn Farm

Courtesy of Lillian Kiernan Brown

Blondie, beloved pet and radio personality

Courtesy of Lena Crain

Bardin Booger in tree
Billy and Lena Crain
Lillian Kiernan Brown and Bardin Booger

Courtesy of Frank Towers, Jr.

Young Frank Towers
Frank Towers with Marie-Therese Lavielle
Frank Towers with Hedva Perahia
Memorial service "*Hommage a* Frank Towers"

Photos by Wanda Glennon Canady

The Granary health-food store
Today's sunrise

Photos by Beth Eifert

Birthday party at Kingsley Lake
Frank Towers at Camp Blanding Museum

Photo by Paula Hilton

Gamin

Photos by Jay Moore

Exterior of Penney Memorial Church

Statue of J.C. Penney

Photos by Jack Rhyne

Cover photo
Shantyboat
Burroughs family home
Black History Museum
Maude Burroughs Jackson

CPSIA information can be obtained
at www.ICGtesting.com
Printed in the USA
FSHW021235120519
58067FS

9 780986 110962